"I am grateful to Danny and Monica for pouring their wisdom, expertise, and experience into this theologically rich and biblically sound resource to help us help kids navigate the many mental health issues they are facing in our broken and challenging world. I can think of no better resource on this topic to prepare us to serve with truth and grace as instruments of hope and healing in our Redeemer's hands."

Walt Mueller, President, The Center for Parent/Youth Understanding

"This timely book by Monica Kim and Danny Kwon is a gift to both parents and ministry leaders. It doesn't shy away from the tough realities of mental health struggles facing the young people we care about, yet it overflows with practical hope about the transformative power of caring, present adults."

Kara Powell, Chief of Leadership Formation, Fuller Seminary; executive director, Fuller Youth Institute; coauthor of *Future-Focused Church*

"Teenagers are a demographic who get talked about a lot but whose care is often overlooked. Danny and Monica have given the church a tremendous gift in this comprehensive but concise handbook to care well and compassionately for the next generation."

Jonathan D. Holmes, Executive Director, Fieldstone Counseling

"Danny and Monica have produced a remarkable resource for parents, pastors, leaders, and volunteers who care about teenagers. It will help them to encourage, pastor, and understand teenagers in their mental health struggles. This book will certainly be on my shelf and should be for everyone who cares about teenagers."

Cameron Cole, Founding Chairman, Rooted Ministry

"Monica Kim and Danny Kwon have given us a long overdue resource for youth leaders, parents, and pastors who often find themselves as first responders when teenagers are struggling. I'm grateful for the thoughtful and practical counsel offered in these pages. This book is a wonderfully thorough resource. It does not shy away from hard questions and tough issues. For anyone who loves teenagers or wants to better equip those who love teenagers, I heartily recommend this resource!"

Duffy Robbins, Professor of Christian Ministry, Grove City College, Grove City, PA

"Grounded in a rich understanding of the good news, this work offers concrete application and true hope for the complex and sometimes tumultuous inner lives of teenagers."

Todd Stryd, MDiv, PsyD, CCEF Faculty; author of *Schizophrenia: A Compassionate Approach*

"As well-versed in psychology as it is rooted in the gospel, this book is a must for anyone who works or lives with teenagers! While informative and practically useful for navigating mental health issues, what I most appreciate is the authors' compassionate stance toward both the one struggling and the ones struggling alongside them."

Kristen Hatton, MA, LPC, Author of *Parenting Ahead: Preparing Now for the Teen Years*

"I'm convinced that Danny and Monica have written the new go-to book for youth workers who want to navigate mental health with sensitivity and biblical faithfulness. You have teenagers in your ministry (or family) who need you to read this book. Don't wait until there's a crisis to open it—read it today."

Mike McGarry, Director of Youth Pastor Theologian; author of *Iconic*, *Discover*, and *Lead Them to Jesus*

"Danny and Monica's decades of faithful, hands-on ministry to teenagers shine through beautifully in this book. Their pastoral and practical wisdom, shaped by deep love for teenagers and their families and grounded in the timeless wisdom of the Word of God will guide, encourage, and help many."

Owen Lee, Senior Pastor, Christ Central Presbyterian Church, Centreville, VA; director, Korean American Leadership Initiative; council member and trustee, SOLA Network

"With a passion for the next generation, Monica Kim and Danny Kwon examine mental health issues from a discipleship perspective, connecting biblically sound principles with practical advice. As experienced ministry professionals, they provide guidance that weaves together the valuable roles played by parents, ministry leaders, the church community, and medical professionals."

Stephen T. Estock, Coordinator, Committee on Discipleship Ministries (CDM), Presbyterian Church in America (PCA)

"As I read through the book, what stood out to me was how Danny and Monica wrote from the perspectives of a pastor, a professional therapist, and parents at different points. There are moments when each voice is exactly what's needed. I'm grateful they poured their experience and wisdom into a resource for both church workers and parents."

Steve S. Chang, President, SOLA Network

Teenagers and Mental Health

....

A Handbook for Parents, Pastors, and Youth Leaders

....

Monica Kim and Danny Kwon

New Growth Press, Greensboro, NC 27401
newgrowthpress.com

All emphases in Scripture references have been added by the author.

Names and identifying details have been changed in vignettes and stories shared.

This book is intended for educational and ministry purposes only; it is not a diagnostic tool. The advice contained here is meant to provide support as you care for and encourage teenagers in the midst of their struggles, not as a substitute for seeking treatment from a qualified medical or counseling professional.

Cover Design: Jamie Keenan
Interior Typesetting and Ebook: Lisa Parnell, lparnellbookservices.com

ISBN: 978-1-64507-551-6 (paperback)
ISBN: 978-1-64507-552-3 (ebook)

Library of Congress Cataloging-in-Publication Data on file

Printed in Colombia

29 28 27 26 25 1 2 3 4 5

To the thousands of loving teenagers and their families whom we have walked with and served, and especially to those striving through mental health challenges. God loves you and so do we.

To our children, who have now grown into young adults. Your journeys from children to teenagers to young adults have taught us so much, and we love you and cherish you. And you all survived your father as your youth pastor!

Contents

Introduction

This book is for anyone who loves and serves teenagers with mental health struggles, from parents, caretakers, mentors, and friends to church leaders, pastors, youth leaders, and volunteers. A variety of struggles fall under the category of mental illness, including schizophrenia, anxiety, bipolar disorder, depression, and attention deficit hyperactivity disorder (ADHD). Our personal journey with teenagers and mental health overlaps with many of these relational and mental health struggles.

Many years ago, an unexpected email from our son's middle school vice principal caught us off guard. Her email notified us that our son was being suspended for passing defamatory notes in class and walking out in the middle of class time. We were shocked because it was inconsistent with what we knew of our child's nature. He was mostly a quiet kid who could sometimes seem shy, but he was social with his group of friends, active in youth group, and always pleasant with others. As far as we knew, most people considered him well-mannered and nice.

At first, I (Danny) was upset. I saw the content of the notes being passed and heard about how my son would just walk out of class, despite his teacher telling him to sit down. My wife (Monica) kept a level head and wanted to seek more understanding about the situation, and she encouraged me to do the same. But it was hard for us to do so because as we often tell parents and caregivers in similar situations, when it's your own child in a crisis, it stirs up many emotions, such as worry, anger, fear, and despair. This was the beginning of our own personal journey with a teenager experiencing a mental health hardship. What started out as a case of school discipline, we were to later discover, was an expression of a profound mental health struggle made worse by the pain of being bullied.

But our journey with mental health issues and teenagers isn't just personal, either. I (Monica) am a psychologist and biblical counselor with twenty years of counseling experience, and I have also taught counseling courses for the Christian Counseling and Educational Foundation (CCEF) and Lehigh University. Until recently, we both served at a large youth and family ministry at one church for twenty-nine years, where Danny was the youth and family pastor. While our experience at one youth group in one church doesn't necessarily validate all our claims, and our experiences may not be applicable to all contexts, our ministry to thousands of students over the course of those twenty-nine years does give us insight into the struggles teenagers face and how parents, pastors, and youth leaders can engage with those experiences in helpful ways.

Over the course of those years working in youth ministry and speaking with countless churches and pastors all over the country, I (Danny) have observed the well-documented rise in mental health struggles in our teenagers and their families. As a result, addressing teen mental health has become an important and necessary part of our ministry. Since the fall of humanity into sin and the suffering that followed, people have struggled with many of these issues, but the significant increase in recent years, particularly during the vulnerable teenage years, has made it more imperative than ever before for the church to minister with wisdom to teens suffering in these ways.

Some claim that the rise in mental health issues is only due to the influence of social media and teenagers who now "self-diagnose" based on what they see online. While there may be some truth to this analysis, evidence has shown a real increase in teenagers' mental health struggles. Recent research indicates that approximately one in five teens between ages twelve and eighteen suffer from at least one diagnosable mental health disorder.[1] Depression and anxiety are also on the rise in teenagers. From 2009 to 2019, the percentage of American teenagers who experienced "persistent feelings of sadness or hopelessness" rose from 26.1 percent to 36.7 percent. Between 2019 and 2021, that number grew to 44.2 percent.[2] This same study also stated that depressive symptoms are up 21 percent in boys and up 50 percent in girls. Another study also found that 75 percent of all anxiety disorders have developed by age twenty-one, and that the median age of onset of anxiety disorders is eleven years old.[3]

Increases in reported poor mental health among the young have coincided with an increase in suicide among the young. For example, in the United States, suicide rates have risen steadily since 2001, according to a recent Centers for Disease Control and Prevention (CDC) report.[4] Various additional studies related to the mental health of teenagers and their struggles show that suicide rates have increased by 76 percent for ages fifteen to nineteen.[5] The highest rate of increase in suicide among all age groups is in kids between ten and fourteen years old.[6]

The COVID–19 pandemic exacerbated mental health issues, but these trends were evident before 2020. For example, the iPhone came out in 2006, which some researchers, such as Jonathan Haidt, point to as one of the beginnings of the increase in mental health issues. However, social media alone does not explain this; other factors such as bullying, parenting issues, violence in schools and media, and social pressures on teenagers have also contributed to the increase.[7]

We have witnessed this trend firsthand. In our first twenty years of ministry at our church, we helped five families seek admission for their teenagers into a local mental health treatment facility. By contrast, in the last nine years, we have had to walk through this painful and difficult process with almost forty teenagers and their families.

Moreover, the number of families seeking our help with a potential mental health issue with their teenager has grown exponentially. (It is important to note that in this book, we use the terms *parents*, *families*, and *caregivers* interchangeably, because we know and minister to numerous teenagers with diverse authority figures and caregivers who are not their birth parents.) Likewise, we have noticed a marked increase in the number of churches that want to consult with us about mental health issues among their teenagers.

Through our combined years of ministry and counseling experience, our hearts have been broken by witnessing the struggles and suffering of teens and their families. Consequently, we do not want them to be at a loss for what to do, so we have combined our expertise to develop protocols and strategies to help them and to guide our church leaders and volunteers in helping them. However, our hearts have been burdened with a desire to not only help the people in our own church and counseling ministry; we desire to also help the many churches and families who face these very same issues. Thus, this book was born. One of its primary goals is to share what we have done in the hope that it can help others in navigating these difficult issues.

One of the titles I (Danny) had considered using for this book was *Everything You Always Wanted to Know About Teenage Mental Health . . . but Were Afraid to Ask*. I am trained as a pastor, not as a psychologist or biblical counselor, but I had the privilege of consulting with Monica about mental health situations that arose at our church over the years. As a result, we could provide informed pastoral care for students and their families in the church, but we also knew when we might need to refer families and students to resources outside the church.

But this wasn't always the case. In the beginning of my work as a youth pastor, I (Danny) would sometimes approach suffering teenagers with beautiful verses like Philippians 4:6–7: "Do not be anxious about anything, but in every situation, by prayer and petition, with thanksgiving, present your requests to God. And the peace of God, which transcends all understanding, will guard your hearts and your minds in Christ Jesus" (NIV). Because I believe this is the absolute truth of God's Word, I just expected them to digest it, embrace it, and live it out. Likewise, I cherished helpful words like these from David Powlison: "Anxiety is the experience that you're all alone in the world that's too big for you. You feel anxious because you can't control your circumstances. But if the Lord is near, everything changes. You aren't alone, and the one who is in control, to order and provide, he is near and he cares for you and he is involved."[8] I thought that if I could just remind people that the Lord is near to them and cares for them, then their mental health struggle would quickly dissipate. I didn't realize at first that Powlison is articulating a deep truth that often needs to be understood over time and in ways particular to the person's suffering. I also didn't realize that there are often multiple layers to mental health struggles that require various approaches, not the generic application of a one-size-fits-all spiritual truth.

Many of you might see yourself in these descriptions, and you might feel nervous even thinking about trying to come alongside a teen struggling in these ways; isn't that something best left to the professionals? There are times when teens need professional help, but parents, pastors, and youth leaders will always have important roles to play in caring for struggling teens. This is true whether we are their primary source of comfort and counsel or whether we get them professional help while providing spiritual and other forms of support for them at home and in the church. We have an amazing opportunity and responsibility to be lovingly patient and long-suffering with our younger brothers and sisters in Christ. As Psalm 34:18 says, "The LORD is near to the brokenhearted and saves the crushed in spirit." To be effective servants of the gospel to teenagers with mental health issues, we need to let them know that we see them and care for them, even as the Lord himself sees them and cares for them. Likewise, if you are a parent or caretaker reading this book, please know God sees you and cares for you, and that churches can be a great source of support and comfort to you as you care for your teen during hard times.

This book is broken down into two major parts. In Part 1, we lay the foundation for the rest of the book. We discuss what the Bible has to say about mental health, the role of the church, teenage development and culture, general principles for caring for teens and their parents, and some considerations for when the situation is beyond the scope of the church. If you are a parent reading this book, Part 1 will help you think biblically about the issue your teen is facing, as well as see ways you could ask the church for more support for either you or your teen.

Part 2 describes broad characteristics of some specific mental health struggles that teenagers face today, including anxiety, depression, eating disorders, substance use issues, trauma, schizophrenia, bipolar disorder, suicidal ideation, and excessive use of screens and social media. Each chapter orients the reader to see the gospel amid the issue, provides a few suggestions for how parents and churches can walk alongside teenagers with those specific struggles, and identifies signs for when additional help might be needed. It is important to note that these chapters are simply an introduction to these issues. While they should provide a helpful biblical orientation and practical strategies for immediately meeting with teens, we highly encourage caregivers to continue reading further about that subject.

Ultimately, our aim is to outline the foundational elements of humble, godly, compassionate care for parents and churches who engage with teenagers struggling with mental illness. Our prayer is that parents, pastors, and youth leaders will be equipped to care in a variety of ways, feel empowered to do so more wisely and skillfully than before, and know when to humbly ask for help from others.

Part 1:

Foundational Principles and Practices for Ministering to Teenagers and Families Dealing with Mental Health Issues

CHAPTER 1

What Does the Bible Say About Mental Health?

All churches have mental health issues within them, whether we know it or not. Research states that one in five adults in the United States struggles with some form of mental health issue.[1] And, as we discussed in the introduction, rates of mental health issues are on the rise, particularly among teens. Many of these people are part of the church, and the church is called to love and care for them. As noted in the introduction, a variety of struggles fall under the category of mental health illness, including such diagnoses as schizophrenia, anxiety, bipolar disorder, and depression.[2]

In our years of ministry, it has always been amazing to see hurting teenagers approach adult leaders in the church to find hope for their complex struggles in the truth of God's Word. I (Danny) saw this firsthand when students in our youth group wanted to make sense of what was going on in their lives and their mental health struggles. While study of Scripture did not automatically remove their struggles or alleviate all their hardships, the life-giving message of the Bible helped them find hope and meaning in their suffering and gave them comfort in the midst of all they were going through.

We will use the terms *mental health*, *mental illness*, or *mental health condition* as a way to distinguish those aspects of our experience from our physical health. When we use the term *mental health professional*, we are generally referring to all those who have additional expertise and training in mental health issues, including biblical counselors, therapists, school psychologists, psychologists, and psychiatrists. God created us as embodied souls, which involves many interrelated processes, so it is not always easy to distinguish between the spiritual, mental, and physical; however, this book will focus primarily on the mental aspects of our experience. Since we are limited in our ability to understand, we place our trust in God, who neither sleeps nor slumbers (Psalm 121:4); we rest in his activity, which allows us to focus on one thing at a time.

The Story of Redemption and Mental Illness

The whole story of redemption in the Bible provides us with a way to understand mental health issues. In Genesis 3, we know all too well that Adam's and Eve's disobedience to God resulted in the fall. And because of the fall, sin has saturated every part of creation, including humanity. The fall has corrupted us, body and soul, and we find ourselves out of harmony with God, ourselves, one another, and the rest of creation. In Romans 3:10–12, Paul quotes Psalm 14:1–3 and Psalm 53:1–3, saying, "As it is written: 'None is righteous, no, not one; no one understands; no one seeks for God. All have turned aside; together they have become worthless; no one does good, not even one.'" Romans 3:23 also explains, "all have sinned and fall short of the glory of God."

As a result of the fall, our embodied estate has become a curse. So we sin and others sin against us. We suffer—ruin, misery, violence, pain, sickness, mental health disorders, disability, aging, and death. However, there is good news—the gospel of Jesus Christ! John 3:16 says, "For God so loved the world, that he gave his only Son, that whoever believes in him should not perish but have eternal life." It is God's love for us that through Jesus we are redeemed from eternal death. Romans 5:17 makes clear that Jesus reversed the curse of death that came through Adam: "For if, because of one man's trespass, death reigned through that one man, much more will those who receive the abundance of grace and the free gift of righteousness reign in life through the one man Jesus Christ."

Now, living in the period after Jesus's death, resurrection, and ascension, we—including believing teenagers—are united to Christ. Through Jesus, we who were separated and far off from Christ have been brought near and made one in Christ (Ephesians 2:12–14). Because of this union, Paul says, "I have been crucified with Christ. It is no longer I who live, but Christ who lives in me" (Galatians 2:20). In our union with Christ, believers live now in communion with him. In union with Christ, our sin and death have been overcome by Christ's righteousness and life. In union with Christ, we are new creations (2 Corinthians 5:17). In union with Christ, all our suffering and hardship will lead to glory with Jesus (Romans 8:17).

Moreover, as Jesus promised, the Holy Spirit was sent in his name (John 14:16–17a, 26a) so now, believers—also believing teenagers—are marked with the seal of the Holy Spirit, indicating our belonging to Christ (Ephesians 1:13). This seal of the Holy Spirit is also a guarantee of our heavenly dwelling that is to come while we live here on earth in our mortal bodies that groan and are burdened (2 Corinthians 5:5).

While we wait for Jesus to return, we will still sin, struggle, and suffer. The believing teenager who lives by faith, will still be under assault from the world (e.g., social media, peer pressure, accessibility of substances), the flesh (e.g., disease, mental health disorders, idolatry, immorality), and the devil (e.g., scheming, deceiving, accusing, lying about God's generosity or goodness and opposing him as he had done in Eden). The Bible makes it clear that there is a battle in us because we live in the overlap of the ages, between the "already" and "not yet." We will live in the struggle with sin—our own and the sin of others against us. We face temptations and weakness (Matthew 26:41), double-mindedness (James 1:8), deceitful hearts (Jeremiah 17:9), suffering (Philippians 1:29), and evil around (1 John 5:19), but because of the hope and strength we have in Jesus, we are called to press on, as the following passages show:

- Watch and pray that you may not enter into temptation. The spirit indeed is willing, but the flesh is weak. (Matthew 26:41)
- You were running well. Who hindered you from obeying the truth? This persuasion is not from him who calls you. . . . But I say, walk by the Spirit, and you will not gratify the desires of the flesh. For the desires of the flesh are against the Spirit, and the desires of the Spirit are against the flesh, for these are opposed to each other, to keep you from doing the things you want to do. (Galatians 5:7–8, 16–17)
- And after you have suffered a little while, the God of all grace, who has called you to his eternal glory in Christ, will himself restore, confirm, strengthen, and establish you. (1 Peter 5:10)
- Finally, be strong in the Lord and in the strength of his might. Put on the whole armor of God, that you may be able to stand against the schemes of the devil. For we do not wrestle against flesh and blood, but against the rulers, against the authorities, against the cosmic powers over this present darkness, against the spiritual forces of evil in the heavenly places. (Ephesians 6:10–12)
- Not that I have already obtained this or am already perfect, but I press on to make it my own, because Christ Jesus has made me his own. Brothers, I do not consider that I have made it my own. But one thing I do: forgetting what lies behind and straining forward to what lies ahead, I press on toward the goal for the prize of the upward call of God in Christ Jesus. Let those of us who are mature think this way, and if in anything you think otherwise, God will reveal that also to you. (Philippians 3:12–15)

The battle against sin and brokenness has been won in Christ, so we are called to persevere and put on the whole armor of God in the battle on earth until our resurrection, which *will* come through our union with Christ. Romans 6:5 encourages us, "For if we have been united with him in a death like his, we shall certainly be united with him in a resurrection like his."

The Christian teenager's mental health struggles stem from both the sin and suffering on this earth. And as Christians, they are called to live by faith, by looking again and again—through each twist, turn, and tumble of any mental health issue—to Jesus who is the founder and perfector of our faith (Hebrews 12:2). *Then*, from faith and the abounding grace of God in Jesus, they aim toward glorifying God and loving their neighbor amid these difficult challenges. As those who care for struggling teenagers, we are called to also live by faith, looking to Jesus again and again—at each twist, turn, and tumble of mental health issues of believing teenagers—*then* from that comfort and assurance that is bound up in God's abounding grace in Christ Jesus, "admonish the idle, encourage the fainthearted, help the weak, be patient with them all" (1 Thessalonians 5:14).

Common Grace and Counseling

In addition to the Bible, God's special revelation, we also believe that God reveals truth through nature, his general revelation (Psalm 19:1–2, Romans 1:19–20), as well as by his common grace (Psalm 145:9, Matthew 5:45). This common grace gives even non-Christians the ability to discern truth. We love this quote from John Calvin, which eloquently describes how we can learn from all people, whether they acknowledge Jesus as Lord or not:

> All truth is from God; and consequently, if wicked men have said anything that is true and just, we ought not to reject it;

> for it has come from God. Therefore, in reading profane authors, the admirable light of truth displayed in them should remind us, that the human mind, however much fallen and perverted from its original integrity, is still adorned, and invested with admirable gifts from its Creator. If we reflect that the Spirit of God is the only fountain of truth, we will be careful, as we would avoid offering insult to him, not to reject or condemn truth wherever it appears.[3]

Because God gives common grace to all people in various ways, we affirm with Calvin that all truth is God's truth, and we do not want to reject it wherever it may be found.

There are some who disagree with us and say that there is no place for insights from secular psychology or biomedical approaches to mental health challenges. However, we believe God's common grace allows secular counselors to make true observations, many of which can be helpful to Christians. David Powlison, who is often considered one of the fathers of the biblical counseling movement, was a primary developer of the Biblical Counseling Coalition's Confessional Statement. In the statement, he and other biblical counseling leaders wrote this about common grace and biblical counseling:

> When we say that Scripture is comprehensive in wisdom, we mean that the Bible makes sense of all things, not that it contains all the information people could ever know about all topics. God's common grace brings many good things to human life. . . . We affirm that numerous sources (such as scientific research, organized observations about human behavior, those we counsel, reflection on our own life experience, literature, film, and history) can contribute to our knowledge of people, and many sources can contribute some relief for the troubles of life.[4]

However, we also affirm that when it comes to non-Christian interpretations and interventions, we do need to exercise caution because although their observations about human nature or the efficacy of various therapeutic techniques may be true, their interpretations and interventions are based on a fundamentally different view of the nature of humanity and the nature of our problems.

At the same time, even Christian counselors may incorporate secular psychology and interpretations to differing degrees. There is ongoing debate among seminaries, Christian universities, Christian counseling organizations, and biblical counselors about how to apply the theology of common grace to secular psychologies when providing Christian counseling. As parents and church leaders, what are we to make of all this? In chapter 4, we recommend that churches develop a list of recommended mental health resources in their communities. This can be incredibly difficult because there is so much variation even within the myriad labels we use. One helpful explanation of the different types of pastoral/biblical counseling and levels of integration of psychology is Tim Keller's article on "Four Models of Counseling in Pastoral Ministry."[5] Another helpful article written by professors at Southeastern Baptist Theological Seminary is titled "What Is Redemptive Counseling/Clinically-Informed Biblical Counseling?" and it outlines a redemptive or clinically-informed approach to biblical counseling, which stands between an integrationist approach and a nouthetic counseling approach (focusing specifically on helping counselees apply biblical wisdom to life).[6]

Ultimately, our aim in this book is not to convince you of a particular approach to mental health care. For our church and youth ministry, it took a great deal of theological reflection, spiritual maturity, and experience to come up with our own approach to biblical, spiritual, and mental health care. Likewise, depending on your theological training and background, your church's theological underpinnings, and your own personal convictions, you might land in a different place than we have. What we suggest is that you would do thorough research as a church. Parents, you can also do your own research as well as talk to leaders in your church. Consider your church's theology to inform your views of counseling and psychology and stay up-to-date about the different types of professional mental health help available in your area.

Key Theological Truths to Hold Onto

Regardless of where you land in terms of how general revelation and common grace informs your understanding of mental health and how to care for people with mental health challenges, we hope that you agree that the Bible does speak to our mental health, and that the church has a role to play in ministering to people struggling with mental health. God's desire for his people is that we would experience total well-being—shalom. However, because of the fall of humanity, we no longer experience uninterrupted peace with God, with one another, or even within ourselves. Even after our hearts are regenerated and our souls are made alive again through our second birth in Christ, much of our experience is marked by discord, not harmony; by brokenness, not wholeness. So, how can we help teens struggling with mental health issues when we who would help them are also suffering sinners? We will discuss various practical ways we can help teens struggling with mental health in chapter 4, but for the remainder of this chapter we will consider the key theological truths we all—parents, pastors, and youth leaders—must hold onto as we carry out this challenging but good work.

We don't go it alone: The Holy Spirit helps us in our weakness

In Romans 8:26–27, Paul says,

> Likewise the Spirit helps us in our weakness. For we do not know what to pray for as we ought, but the Spirit himself

> intercedes for us with groanings too deep for words. And he who searches hearts knows what is the mind of the Spirit, because the Spirit intercedes for the saints according to the will of God.

None of the children of God go it alone, even if the circumstances and the pain of suffering seem to scream otherwise. And Paul says the "Spirit of him who raised Jesus from the dead" is the same Spirit who dwells in the children of God (Romans 8:11). The Spirit is powerfully active, concrete, and real, *not* simply an empowering agent or feeling. We do not go it alone!

It is amazing to us how God helps us in our ministry to teenagers and even how he helped us with our own teenager who had mental health struggles. I thank the Lord for the times he prompts me to check in on a struggling student by texting encouragement from Scripture. Or the times God will remind me of a student who has been seeking counseling outside the church and prompts me to set up a time to grab a meal with them. Likewise, in a church pastoral staff meeting, a colleague will ask about a family, and it will remind me to reach out to and care for the parents of a struggling teenager. In distinct and diverse ways, God is always active and real and does not leave us alone in caring for teenagers and families in need.

We are prone to judgmentalism: God wants us to examine our hearts

Another foundational element of compassionate care is the self-awareness of parents and those in the church who minister to teenagers. You might have a hard time being patient with every teenager or caregiver. Sometimes you may have an easier time being patient with teenagers, but not equally so with the caregivers. Many times, as parents dealing with our own teenagers, patience and compassion can even feel impossible. Without self-awareness, our instinctive thoughts about and reactions to teenagers' struggles or their parents' issues can get in the way!

It's important to pray and reflect, asking God to reveal our hearts. We can start by praying, "Search me, O God, and know my heart; test me and know my anxious thoughts. See if there is any offensive way in me, and lead me in the way everlasting" (Psalm 139:23–24 NIV). Because the Holy Spirit dwells in us, God can reveal to us our anxious hearts. So we appeal to God, who knows us intimately, for deeper self-awareness.

As we pray about our heart issues, we must also guard against a judgmental, hypocritical spirit. As Jesus says in Matthew 7:1–5,

> Judge not, that you be not judged. For with the judgment you pronounce you will be judged, and with the measure you use it will be measured to you. Why do you see the speck that is in your brother's eye, but do not notice the log that is in your own eye? Or how can you say to your brother, "Let me take the speck out of your eye," when there is the log in your own eye? You hypocrite, first take the log out of your own eye, and then you will see clearly to take the speck out of your brother's eye.

As we seek to be the means that God uses to remove the "speck" in our brother's eye, we must continually be dealing with the logs jammed in our own eyes. Only then can we obey Jesus's command to "not judge by appearances, but judge with right judgment" (John 7:24) and speak with the wisdom that comes from above (James 3:17).

We have hope: The promise of future glory helps us persevere

Holding onto our eternal hope as we minister to people struggling with mental illness is essential. They will need us to lovingly and wisely point them to our future hope, and we will need to remind ourselves of it again and again as we are tempted to despair and discouragement when change is slow or nonexistent. In Romans 8:18–25, Paul helps us view the suffering of this present time in light of the hope of glory, the redemption of our bodies for those who are in Christ Jesus. Although our suffering is real (and Paul certainly knew what it was like to suffer), Paul considers how our present suffering pales in comparison to this hope of glory for those who have been saved and sealed with the Holy Spirit:

> For I consider that the sufferings of this present time are not worth comparing with the glory that is to be revealed to us. For the creation waits with eager longing for the revealing of the sons of God. For the creation was subjected to futility, not willingly, but because of him who subjected it, in hope that the creation itself will be set free from its bondage to corruption and obtain the freedom of the glory of the children of God. For we know that the whole creation has been groaning together in the pains of childbirth until now. And not only the creation, but we ourselves, who have the firstfruits of the Spirit, groan inwardly as we wait eagerly for adoption as sons, the redemption of our bodies. For in this hope we were saved. Now hope that is seen is not hope. For who hopes for what he sees? But if we hope for what we do not see, we wait for it with patience.

This hope of glory and redemption from this body of suffering—including our mental health suffering—is deeply important for us all to grasp. Sometimes, sufferings and mental health hardships don't resolve quickly—it can be a journey that lasts quite a while, even until we see Jesus face-to-face. In addition, while walking alongside teenagers and their caregivers on the journey, we might even witness more severe mental health conditions develop.

This journey can prove to be more treacherous than expected, and we or those we minister to will at times feel hopeless.

We want this kind of glory now, but we must learn how to patiently hold onto hope for future, presently unseen glory. This is an important part of what it means to walk by faith. Hebrews 11:1 tells us, "Now faith is the assurance of things hoped for, the conviction of things not seen." The rest of Hebrews 11 then gives us example after example of how people of faith believed in the unseen, of how they looked to the future with hope. This does not mean that we should feel ashamed of our discouragement and despair; as the Psalms, Lamentations, Job, and many other places in Scripture teach us, we can honestly voice those very real feelings to God. However, especially as those seeking to help others, we must continually remind ourselves of the reality of our future hope, so that we can faithfully obey the command to "Rejoice in hope, be patient in tribulation, be constant in prayer" (Romans 12:12). We cannot offer anything to others that we have not first received ourselves.

CHAPTER 2

What Is the Role of the Church in Addressing Teen Mental Health?

Proverbs 16:21–22 says, "The wise of heart is called discerning, and sweetness of speech increases persuasiveness. Good sense is a fountain of life to him who has it, but the instruction of fools is folly." These verses remind us of the importance and power of wisdom. Over the years, we have realized that one of the most difficult things to navigate about teenagers and mental health is knowing when a church should get involved. This requires wisdom. For example, in our church, sometimes we have sensed something strange or peculiar with a student, but we weren't certain that there was a mental health issue. In these situations, pastors or youth leaders might wonder if they should ask the family about their teenager. And if so, how do you approach a caregiver or parent if you suspect a mental health issue?

Developing a Relationship with Teenagers' Families

It can be incredibly awkward to suddenly approach a family about their teenager. Mental health issues are very sensitive for families. Bringing up even the possibility of mental illness in their teen can stir a range of strong emotions, including fear, worry, panic, distress, alarm, embarrassment, and shame. Pastors, if you haven't started already, we would suggest developing a caring pastoral presence not only with the teenagers in your church or youth ministry (if your church has a youth ministry) but also with their caregivers.

We strongly advocate for youth ministry to be a family-centric, intergenerational partnership with parents and families. This can take the form of active communication with parents by sending them updates and newsletters about the youth ministry. This could also mean providing resources or equipping opportunities for parents and families to help them care for their teenagers (we will provide some examples of what this could look like later). These kinds of care and events not only provide help for caregivers but build relationships between church leaders and caregivers. Hence, if or when a potential mental health issue arises, there is already a built-in relational dynamic and trust.

When and how to reach out to parents or caregivers about a potential mental health issue in their teenager is a matter of careful discernment, balancing the context of the family in question with the real (sometimes emergency-level) needs of the student. A direct approach can elicit various negative responses, ranging from defensiveness to insecurity to anger to feelings of intrusiveness. As a younger pastor in my church, I (Danny) blundered in this area a few times. Even the best reactions from parents often include their initial feelings of exposure and shame, which we try to avoid as much as possible, as it hinders their openness to receiving help.

Instead, we suggest that church leaders approach families with a posture of care blended with curiosity, perhaps over coffee or a meal, asking non-intrusive questions:

- "I have noticed…"
- "How is your child doing with…"
- "Is there anything I can do to help right now?"
- "Do you have any present concerns or worries about your teenager?"

Open-ended questions such as these might help parents recognize the patterns you have noticed or bolster their willingness to talk about concerns they have also noticed. Regardless of what they do or don't share, make sure to offer your love and help to the families and parents by saying things like, "Is there anything I can do to minister to your child?" or "How can I support you in your role as a parent?" These questions are non-threatening ways you can open up the possibility for conversation about the teens' mental health and express your support and love for them as a family. In our ministry, we have found three metaphors for our role to be very helpful in capturing what the church can offer to teens struggling with mental health issues.

Refuge

One way that churches and youth ministries can serve teenagers and families is by being a place of refuge. Scripture teaches the idea that a refuge is a place to seek protection and put one's trust in. Psalm 46:1 states that "God is our refuge and strength, a very present help in trouble." This conveys the idea of a place of safety, aid, and relief. As the body of Christ, this is what churches and youth ministries can be for families and teenagers facing mental health issues.

Mental health struggles can be bewildering for teenagers and their families. They can elicit feelings of uncertainty, doubt, worry, and fear, both for the struggling teenager as well as for the families learning how to support and help them. Knowing that our church is a refuge can be a great comfort. Not all teenagers and families will seek to find refuge in their churches. However, churches and youth ministries can make every effort to ensure that they are a welcoming refuge of unconditional love for families, pointing them to God, our ultimate refuge and strength who is always with us, no matter how troubling the situation.

Lighthouse

A lighthouse is another metaphor that can inform the way the church interacts with teens struggling with mental health issues.

A lighthouse is a tower designed to project light and to serve as a navigational aid. Psalm 27:1 says, "The LORD is my light and my salvation; whom shall I fear? The LORD is the stronghold of my life; of whom shall I be afraid?" And because we have the Holy Spirit in us, we are "the light of the world" who ought to let our "light shine before others" (Matthew 5:14, 16).

For our church and youth ministry, the lighthouse has become symbolic of our philosophy of ministry in helping teenagers and families struggling with mental health issues. We hope to be a navigational aid, helping them make their way through dangerous waters. This does not mean that we know all the answers or can provide all the resources for teenagers and their families. However, we can seek to provide guidance and help.

First responder

Finally, the last picture of how churches and youth ministries can serve families and teenagers is the concept of being a first responder, which is a concept that a youth pastor friend of ours frequently uses in his ministry to teenagers. Traditionally, a first responder can be defined as a person with training who is among the first to arrive and provide assistance or incident resolution at the scene of an emergency. While a first responder may not be able to provide long-term care or help, they are there to help with the initial responses to an emergency. When it comes to mental health and teenagers, churches and youth ministries might not be able to provide the proper long-term help, or at least not all the kinds of long-term help that might be needed, but they can provide initial assistance to families and teenagers in mental health crises. This can be anything from being a place of comfort and solace for a family to providing direction and resources for a family to seek further help. The important thing is that families and teenagers know that their church and youth ministry are a source of help. Psalm 3:1–4 presents a picture of how the Lord responds to David's cries for help. As we look to the Lord for help and rescue in our own lives, he empowers us to join him in offering help to those in our youth ministries and churches.

Practical Tools for Families and Teenagers

While the metaphors of refuge, lighthouse, and first responder can provide guiding pictures of the church's role in engaging with teens' mental health struggles, it's important to consider what this might look like in practice. In chapters 4 and 5 we will discuss specific ways churches can care for teens and their parents, but in this chapter, we will consider a few big-picture ways that churches can be a refuge, lighthouse, or first responder.

Raise awareness by talking openly and honestly about mental health

Churches and youth ministries can be a lighthouse by proactively demonstrating that they care about the mental health of teenagers. Of course, we need to let families know that churches do not have all the answers or solutions, but we can be a refuge for them. Moreover, keeping families and teenagers informed and letting them know we are aware and care about potential mental health issues can be done in various ways, so that they know it is safe to reach out to us as their "first responders" if a crisis arises.

As we raise awareness, it is important to be authentic and open about mental health, because one of the biggest struggles with mental health issues is the stigma and shame that they bring. By talking openly about them in your church, you provide a forum of gospel love and unconditional acceptance for students and their families, letting them know that they are not weird, strange, or alone in their journey, nor do they need to feel ashamed or hide their struggles.

It is also important to talk openly about it so that fellow teenagers can learn to love, accept, and care for those who might have mental health struggles. Jesus said he was the great physician who came for the sick. In the same way, our teenagers at church can live out this calling of Jesus by modeling his love, care, and openness to students with mental illness. But first it must be an open and authentic issue in your church and youth ministry.

Years ago, we had a student with a mental illness that caused her to be somewhat disruptive during youth group, especially during teaching or prayer times. Her outbursts distracted many students and agitated many of our adult leaders. Moreover, some parents even complained to our church leaders about this teenager and how she was being disruptive to the youth ministry meetings. Some parents considered not bringing their teens to youth group anymore, and other parents said that there needed to be more direct supervision of this student to keep her quiet.

However, our church and youth ministry had a two-fold response. First, our conviction was that everyone, even students with mental health issues, needed to hear the gospel. No matter their struggle, our youth group needed to be an environment where all could come openly and unconditionally to hear the gospel. Second, our teenagers (and also our adult volunteers) needed to grow in practicing love, compassion, and grace for others. We would not discriminate against someone because of a mental illness. Rather, we would practice love and care for them. We did not ignore the concerns parents expressed, but instead we found ways for some of the other teenagers to serve this student and care for her, as well as ways leaders could help this teenager be more involved in youth group meetings to help reduce the disruptions of her outbursts. Having open, honest conversations about mental health also means we need to be prepared to live out the realities of loving teens with mental health issues in our churches.

Provide workshops for families and caregivers

Periodically, we can engage with parents by offering workshops or seminars for them on the mental health issues of their teenagers. The topics can vary from anxiety and stress to more nuanced topics like how to deal with a potential social media addiction. It is not so much the topic that is important; by providing teaching on mental health topics, families in your church will know that you care about these issues, are open to hearing about any potential struggle they or their teens might have, and are willing to equip them in these struggles.

Partnering and walking alongside parents is part of the calling of the church. Deuteronomy 6:4–9 describes the importance of the community of God serving together to instruct the young generation. Likewise, in Mark 3:35, Jesus points to the family of God as those united by doing the will of God. Finally, in 1 Peter 4:10, it instructs us to use our gifts to serve one another. In this way, parents should not be isolated in raising and discipling their children. Rather, there is a biblical calling for churches as a community to partner with parents in equipping and helping them to raise up children and teenagers.

Discuss care and treatment options

Churches and youth ministries can consult with parents when their teens are struggling with mental health issues and help them identify the various resources available to them in their particular community. At our church, we curated a list of reliable counseling services, which can be especially helpful if your church is limited in terms of the ongoing counseling support it can provide. We not only offer it to parents and caregivers but also discuss with them the pros and cons of the various options on the list. Likewise, we offer to go with families to talk with a mental health professional, a pediatrician, or their school counselors if they wish.

We all know that the church's primary mission is to minister to people spiritually, but the church can also play an important role in providing for people's physical and psychological needs, even if it means referring them to further resources when those needs go beyond what the church is equipped to provide. As James 2:15–16 says,

"If a brother or sister is poorly clothed and lacking in daily food, and one of you says to them, 'Go in peace, be warmed and filled,' without giving them the things needed for the body, what good is that?" Let's be creative about how we can practically come alongside suffering teens and their families so that we might love them not just "in word or talk but in deed and in truth" (1 John 3:18).

Educate the teenagers in your church

Teenagers need to know that the church is aware of and cares about their mental health issues. Whether it is discussing proactive care to prevent issues from arising or responsive care for those who are struggling, when we talk honestly about mental health, it benefits everyone. At our church, we offer workshops and seminars both from me (Monica) and from outside speakers, covering topics such as social media, anxiety, and academic pressure, as well as a variety of other topics geared toward our teenagers. These times not only minister to our teenagers directly but also serve to support the parents, who see our investment in teaching about these issues and know that we care about them and are here to help them. As the apostle Paul calls the church to teach and admonish one another in Colossians 3:16, we do so also through the vehicle of biblically informed mental health education.

Offer to visit teenagers

In Romans 12:13, Paul instructs the church to contribute to the needs of the saints and show hospitality. When it comes to the mental health struggles of teenagers in the church, this can be done through one-on-one time with a teenager. For example, if a caregiver raises a concern about their teenager's mental health, we discreetly offer to do a "hang out" to meet with their student, usually over a series of a few meetings. This can also give pastors and youth leaders the chance to get to know the student more and assess their situation. It is important to be clear to families and parents that the church cannot diagnose mental health disorders or offer medical treatments, but as first responders we can help parents discern what might be going on and point them to additional resources when necessary.

Provide service opportunities

For teenagers with mental health struggles, social settings like youth ministry events can be a challenge. It can also be hard for parents to observe or hear how challenging these situations are. Likewise, fellow youth group members might be uncomfortable with their friends' struggles for various reasons. A former student struggled with anxiety, especially when she was around others, and she would go completely into a shell when she came to youth group. At times during small group, she would just stare at the ground and not respond to anyone talking to her, go into a corner of the room and sit by herself, or leave the room abruptly.

We definitely wanted to respect and give space to this teenager. Generally, we want to give each student struggling with mental health the time they need to grow and heal. But for the parents, this not only caused concern; it was heartbreaking. Yet, there were two things we knew we could do for this teenager. First, we had to equip fellow youth group members and adult leaders so they knew how to relate to the struggling teenager and how to include her into the group. Sometimes, this meant having one student go care for her when she left due to her anxiety. At other times, it was just making them aware of how anxiety was impacting this student. And from time to time, it meant educating the group on how to make this student feel more welcome and comfortable.

Second, we wanted to help this student by giving her opportunities to take an active role in the group, versus feeling isolated and letting her anxiety overtake her. We gave her chances to read Scripture, asked her to lead one part of the discussion sometimes, and eventually even had her take part in contacting students each week to remind them of their small group meetings. In each of these ways, we were able to equip her and help her know that she is a valuable member of the body of Christ and that God has given her gifts that she can use for his service. Even if it is difficult at times, finding ways to incorporate teens struggling with mental health issues into serving the body of Christ can be an important way the church ministers to them. First Corinthians 12:21–26 reminds us of the importance and value of every member of the body of Christ, and how important it is to find ways to uplift them, even those with mental health struggles.

Cultivate a place of belonging

In addition to incorporating struggling teens into the life of the church through service opportunities, as leaders we can help our churches be places of refuge by cultivating a place of belonging for students who are struggling. Ephesians 2:19 reminds us, "So then you are no longer strangers and aliens, but you are fellow citizens with the saints and members of the household of God." We want our teens to feel this sense of belonging and know that they are fellow citizens, members of the household of God.

We have had several students with severe mental health issues who had to leave their schools for a period of time for either outpatient or inpatient care. For teens, leaving your school and your friends can feel devastating. For parents, the transitions in and out of schools can be a huge cause of worry and concern. Other students often wonder why they left school, look strangely at them and their situation, and even ostracize them. The church and youth ministry, however, can be a place where they do not have labels. In fact, rather than any labels, they can feel a place of safety and belonging in their churches and youth ministries as we seek to live out the gospel with one another as described in passages like Romans 12:9–21 or 1 Corinthians 13:4–7.

Be sensitive with youth group activities and programs

Youth group activities like icebreakers, group games, or open gym time might be difficult for a student struggling with a mental health issue; these are not necessarily things we should stop doing, but it is something to be aware of so we can offer alternatives and ensure we are providing a variety of ways for teens to engage with one another and with the leaders. We recall a student who struggled with anxiety, but who seemed to participate in many of our youth group games and activities. He later shared how fearful and stressful it was for him to do activities with others at youth group. And after a bit of time had passed, he came to Monica to share his deep discomfort and stress in doing many of these activities, even though he had participated in them for a while. It was something I (Danny), as the youth leader, had no idea about. However, after this teenager talked with my wife and then we all talked about it together, we immediately found other ways he could be involved. It was amazing to see how much his disposition and cheerfulness changed at the youth group because we recognized his struggle and tried to care for him through it.

Parents, if your teenager struggles with youth group programs and activities, don't be afraid to talk to your youth leaders about it. Pastors and youth leaders may not always immediately know what or how we need to do things differently, but when we become aware of the issue, we can be creative about finding other ways to minister to and engage the unique teens God has placed within our church.

Seek accountability and counsel

As we seek to care for the teens in our church struggling with mental health issues, it's important to involve others, both for accountability and for advice as these situations unfold. Proverbs 15:22 reminds us of the importance of wise counsel and advisers. This must be done respecting confidentiality and respect for the teenager and their family. Yet, due to the serious nature of mental health issues, it is prudent to keep a pastor, elder, deacon, or other trusted member of the church aware of the help you are providing. This is to safeguard the helper and also to keep them accountable to someone for consultation and advice if needed, and in the worst-case scenario, to help if any liability issues were to arise. Usually, parents are encouraged to know that there is more than one person in leadership whom they can reach out to about the church's care for their teenager.

In addition to seeking accountability for ourselves as church leaders, caring for the parents of struggling teens also comes in the form of providing accountability to them. While we want to be gentle with the families and caregivers coming to us for help, we also must not forget the church's prophetic role of speaking truth to power, and parents hold an incredibly powerful, God-given role of authority in their teens' lives (Colossians 3:20; Ephesians 6:1). Sometimes this means we might need to gracefully challenge caregivers on some of the decisions they are making or how their actions are impacting their teenager.

In our youth ministry, Monica often uses the phrase "be the parent" to the caregivers of teenagers. While we always use these words gently, it is our way of reminding parents that at the end of the day, they are the adults in this relationship. And while their role as an authoritative adult in their teen's life might be burdensome, stressful, or difficult, especially in the context of mental illness, God has called them to model God as Father to their children. This means that as parents or caregivers, we are called to be stronger than our children (not emotionally fragile and reactive), wiser than our children (not foolishly rash or immature), and full of abundant, sacrificial love (not demanding love from them or selfishly expecting them to make our lives easier or better).

The perfections of God the Father are a high standard to imitate! Instead of pursuing this goal, we may be tempted to aim for a more attainable, human model of "good parenting." But instead of lowering the standard, a better response is to humbly admit that none of us is sufficient for these things, graciously receive the help and wisdom of others, repent to our teens and to God each time we fall short, and pray for the power of the Holy Spirit to grow in becoming more like our loving, stable heavenly Father, "with whom there is no variation or shadow due to change" (James 1:17) and who is abundantly "kind to the ungrateful and the evil" (Luke 6:35).

Walking with Suffering Saints

As we consider throughout the rest of this book how to best care for teens with mental health issues, it's important to remember that mental illness always involves suffering even though there is also sin. And with teenagers, it involves not only their suffering, but also the suffering of their caregivers. Teens might feel alone while enduring great agony. They might feel ashamed to talk to anyone about their struggle. And for parents, they may blame themselves for their teens' struggles or fear the judgment of others. We must seek to walk alongside suffering teens and their suffering parents with tenderness and patience.

All churches contain people struggling with mental health issues. It is the responsibility of the church to care for these suffering saints, whether teens or adults. Thus, we must grow in wisdom in how to do this well, particularly for teens, who are increasingly struggling with mental health issues. We can do this through the power of the Holy Spirit as we nurture a gathering of believers that serves and helps this ever-present population in our churches. In doing so, parents, pastors, and youth leaders can journey together in helping our young brothers and sisters in Christ grow into maturity in the faith as they experience trials of various kinds.

CHAPTER 3

Teenage Development and Culture

As we have served thousands of teenagers over the course of our ministry, we have found it invaluable to understand some unique aspects of their developmental stage (their "creatureliness") and current teenage culture. The gospel never changes, but culture does. Part of faithfully proclaiming the Word and making disciples is doing the hard, creative work of considering how to best communicate the eternal truths of Scripture in ways that our listeners can hear and understand. And when it comes to practical care, it is important to understand the specific needs of those we care so we can be of real help.

Our hope is that as you reflect on a few relevant aspects of teenagers' development and culture, you can use all this information in a kingdom-minded way. The kingdom of God is indeed at hand and has come through Jesus. Although teenagers may suffer from acute mental health conditions even to the point of death, pressing into this eternal hope enables those who love teenagers not to dismiss or diminish their suffering, but to soberly face and compassionately care for them. Because of this already and eternal truth of the kingdom of God, those who care for teenagers in mental health crises can be quick to listen and slow to speak (James 1:19). We slow down and become curiously concerned in a humble way to understand how teenagers and their families have suffered through their mental health struggles. We can be more thoughtful about when and how we pray, resting in the knowledge that we have a great high priest interceding for us in heaven (Hebrews 7:23–28), and when we don't know how to pray, the Holy Spirit "intercedes for us with groanings too deep for words" (Romans 8:26).

Adolescent Development: Reflecting our Creatureliness

It's not unusual for adults to forget what it was like to be a teenager, and so we expect them to think and behave like adults. We can easily become frustrated or perplexed when teenagers don't think and act in a manner we want, and we can even use the Bible to shame them. When mental health struggles start to emerge, we want them to quickly master self-control over their unhelpful thoughts and emotions. In 1 Corinthians 13:11–12, Paul says, "When I was a child, I spoke like a child, I thought like a child, I reasoned like a child. When I became a man, I gave up childish ways." Paul uses this to illustrate turning away from things that are passing away and turning toward what is eternal; he continues by saying, "For now we see in a mirror dimly, but then face to face. Now I know in part; then I shall know fully, even as I have been fully known." There is much that can be said regarding the central message of this passage, but that is not the focus of this chapter. For this chapter, it is important to notice that although the Bible is not a book about the stages of human development, Paul uses this common knowledge for his purposes. It is common knowledge that there are differences and distinctions in human developmental stages—whether one is an infant, toddler, teen, young adult, adult, or older adult. This common knowledge is important to understand when caring for a teenager.

Growth and development happen from infancy to adulthood. These changes are progressive—happening over a period of time—and are an important part of our creatureliness. Growth and development from infancy onward have always been part of God's masterful plan as our Creator, who, after creating human beings—male and female—said to them in Genesis 1:28, "Be fruitful and multiply." Although the Bible does not provide much information about how Jesus went through these stages of development, we know that Jesus, being fully human and fully God, did go through these stages—albeit perfectly and without blemish. We can read in the Bible about Jesus as a baby and Jesus at age twelve and marvel at the mystery of the eternal Son increasing "in wisdom and in stature and in favor with God and man" (Luke 2:52).

Although he was using it as an illustration, Paul provides an accurate description of how being a child is like having an experience of looking into a mirror and seeing things dimly, compared to the more clear-sighted vision of an adult. As adults, we can certainly identify with this description. We often have thoughts like, *If only I (Monica) understood this when I was a teenager, then things could have been different.* I'm sure I'm not the only one who at some point has thought about regrets when looking back at those dimly lit teenage years. For most teenagers, there are certain ranges of developmental features that cannot be forced ahead, even if one wishes it were so—if one is a child, one can only speak, think, and reason like a child; teens can only speak, think, and reason like a teen. The goal is to grow in maturity, but we must recognize the reality of developmental stages.

There have been many thoughtful theorists and researchers who have examined the matters of human development and have identified various distinct stages in development. Understanding some of this information can help those who love teenagers and are near to them—parents, pastors, youth leaders, and volunteers—to know how to care for teens in a humble, compassionate, and wise manner.

Because God is our all-wise Creator, we are dependent on his masterful work to grow us from infancy to adulthood, even though we speak predominantly in terms of biological and behavioral changes that happen. According to developmental theories and research, these are generally agreed-upon developmental stages broken down by age:

- Infancy: birth to 24 months
- Early childhood: 2–5 or 6—the preschool years
- Middle and late childhood: 6–11
- **Adolescence: 10–12 through 18–21—after puberty**
- Early adulthood: 20s–30s
- Middle adulthood: 40s–60s
- Late adulthood: 60s or 70s through death

Please understand that these ages are not fixed—people can be in different developmental stages than their age might lead you to expect based on a variety of factors. As a related aside, it is interesting to make a note of how in various passages in the Old Testament, men who were twenty years old and older were included in a census and were considered able to fight in the army (e.g., Numbers 1:45), but not those under twenty. Although physically many teens are fully mature, God's law in the Bible recognizes that there is a difference between a physically mature sixteen-year-old and a twenty-year-old.

Adolescence: The Transition Between Childhood and Adulthood

Adolescence is a period of transition between childhood and adulthood. It is commonly understood that adolescence is a sensitive period in which substantial changes and developments happen, such as physical maturation, brain development, and a drive for independence, developing a sense of identity, and the increased influence of social and peer interactions. Some have called this the "storm and stress" period. Physically, the adolescent stage reaches peak maturity; it is the healthiest time of life. During this period, there are improvements in strength, speed, reaction time, immune function, and reasoning. Additionally, there is an increased resistance to many types of injury. It can be a truly remarkable period.

Having gone on many humanitarian/mission-vision trips with teenagers over the course of our twenty-nine years in youth and family ministry, I (Monica) witnessed how God used teenagers in amazing ways while partnering with other local youths in various communities. They not only quickly developed genuine friendships, enabling them to engage in rich conversations about the gospel, but they also built foundations for schools, installed large tanks for rainwater collection and storage, and cleared vast fields of weeds to get them ready for planting crops for a small village, to name a few—all with an adult guide, of course. They were remarkable. I still look back in wonder and amazement at how God used the physical vitality of teens to bring encouragement to many people—those who knew Jesus and those who didn't.

Yet for some, adolescence can also be quite hazardous due to substance use issues (e.g., alcohol, nicotine, cannabis, and other illicit drugs), sexually transmitted infections, accidents, suicide, or even homicide. It can be a time of great opportunity but also great risk. During the adolescent years, the brain develops in stages; different parts of the brain mature at different times. The front part of the brain (i.e., prefrontal cortex) that exercises cognitive control (e.g., performing goal-directed tasks, inhibiting impulsiveness, assessing risk in decisions, and regulating emotions) continues to mature from childhood to young adulthood. It is one of the last parts of the brain to mature; it continues to develop into the mid- to late-twenties.[1]

However, other parts of the adolescent brain develop sooner, like the areas that are linked to sensory and motor tasks, the emotional processing center (i.e., limbic system), and the reward center (i.e., nucleus accumbens), which is critical in detecting and learning about new and rewarding cues in the environment. The differently developing parts of the brain during the adolescent period may create an imbalance, such that in an emotionally laden situation, the emotion and reward centers may be more activated than the less mature cognitive control part of the brain. Furthermore, the social context, especially when it involves peers, can function as a rewarding or motivational cue in the environment that can impact cognitive control, either positively or negatively. Rewards can increase or decrease goal-directed behaviors. So, this imbalance between cognitive and affective processes can increase the temptation to make riskier choices. Additionally, research into the developing teenage brain highlights how fine-tuning of the connections between various parts of the motivational-emotional regions with various parts of the cognitive control region of the brain are happening at different rates too.[2] These interconnections continue to develop until young adulthood and can impact regulation of emotional reactions and self-control. What this means is that teenagers may be more susceptible to emotional highs and lows, and they may decide to try things that involve more risks, particularly when there are notable rewards from the emotionally laden situation or from peers.

All of this does not mean, however, that teenagers are *unable* to make reasonable decisions. In addition, the processes in the brain, while better understood now than they have been in the past, are still very complex. Continual growth in learning how to manage their emotions and exercising self-control are vital goals during these years. Not only can pursuing these goals open up opportunities for deepening a teenager's relationship with Jesus because of grace, but scriptural promises, when applied wisely and faithfully, can provide living hope, comfort, and a way through for teenagers struggling with mental health issues. In this, we are reminded of 2 Corinthians 5:4, which says, "For while we are still in this tent, we groan, being burdened—not that we would be unclothed, but that we would be further clothed, so that what is mortal may be swallowed up by life."

As we continue to learn more about teenagers' brain development, we cannot be reductionistic and boil down adolescent behavior solely to expressions of their developing brains, because it also involves deceitful desires (Ephesians 4:22)—it is a both/and. Furthermore, we cannot know every detail of God's creation, and so we marvel at God's infiniteness as Psalm 90:2 declares, "Before the mountains were brought forth, or ever you had formed the earth and the world, from everlasting to everlasting you are God." We must humbly acknowledge that his thoughts and ways are higher than ours (Isaiah 55:8–9), even as we aim to grow in understanding.

Adolescence: Risk-Taking and Emergence of Mental Illness

Adolescence is also marked by increased mortality rates, with accidents, homicide, and suicide being the three leading causes of death among teenagers, according to the CDC. Risky behaviors such as substance use, unsafe sexual activity, and reckless decision-making also peak during this stage. According to the CDC, the following statistics reflect ten-year trends among high school students between 2013 and 2023:[3]

- 32% have had sex (a decrease from 47% in 2013)
- 21% are currently sexually active (a decrease from 34% in 2013)
- 22% currently drink alcohol (down from 35% in 2013)
- 17% currently use marijuana (a decrease from 23% in 2013)
- 18% currently use an electronic vapor product
- 16% have been cyberbullied, with 21% of female students and 12% of male students reporting this (the percentage of total that were cyberbullied has remained relatively consistent since 2013)
- 19% have been bullied at school (this percentage has remained relatively consistent since 2013)
- 9% have been threatened or injured with a weapon at school (up from 7% in 2013)
- 11% have experienced sexual violence by anyone, with 18% of female students having experienced sexual violence by anyone (the total percentage was 10% in 2017 when this concern was added to the research)
- 9% have been forced to have sex, with 14% of female students reported having ever been forced to have sex (7% was reported in 2013)

- 40% have experienced persistent sadness or hopelessness almost every day for two weeks or more in a row, with 53% of female students reporting this (the total percentage is an increase from 30% reported in 2013)
- 29% have experienced poor mental health (this percentage remained consistent with the reporting in 2021 when the CDC began tracking this issue)
- 20% have seriously considered attempting suicide, 16% have made a suicide plan, and 9% have attempted it (these numbers reflect an increase from 2013 when 17% have seriously considered attempting suicide, 14% have made a plan, and 8% have attempted)

In addition to risky behaviors, mental illnesses often emerge during adolescence. Figure 1 is a graph produced by Casey and colleagues,[4] who have conducted an array of research on the developing adolescent brain. This graph depicts which mental illnesses emerge and peak during adolescence. We want to make it clear, however, that mental illnesses are not simply caused by all these transitions and changes in the brain-body that are happening during the adolescent stage.

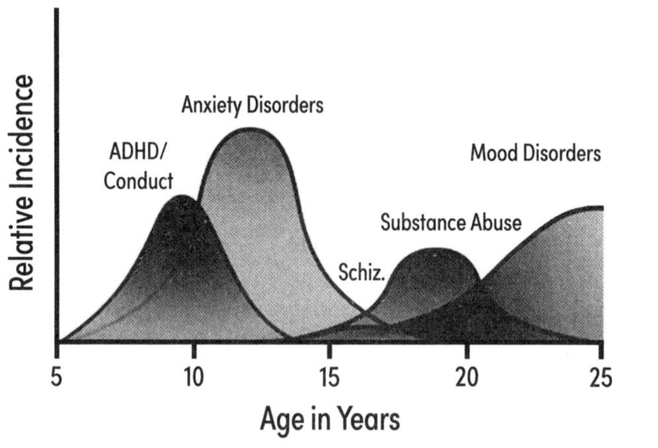

Figure 1: Mental health illnesses emerge and peak during adolescence

And yet, it is important to recognize that adolescence is a period of heightened emotional reactivity, and some teens who are not able to manage their heightened emotional reactivity consistently over a period of time are at greater risk for mental illnesses, such as anxiety or depression, to emerge. According to the CDC,[5] while "mental health encompasses a range of mental, emotional, social, and behavioral functioning and occurs along a continuum from good to poor," some of the most common mental health issues children and teenagers face are ADHD, anxiety, and depression. They found that about 10 percent of all children and teenagers aged three to seventeen struggle with ADHD, 9.5 percent of teenagers experience anxiety that interferes with their everyday functioning, and around 4.5 percent live with depression. According to the National Alliance on Mental Illness (NAMI), one in six US youths aged six to seventeen experience a mental health disorder each year and 50 percent of all lifetime mental illness begins by age fourteen, and 75 percent by age twenty-four.[6]

The ability of teenagers to regulate emotions and exercise self-control is one of the more important developmental tasks during the teenage years. A lot of research examining the adolescent stage emphasizes that persistent emotional dysregulation is one of the stronger risk factors for the development of mental illnesses.[7] Emotional dysregulation is understood as the inability to modulate the intensity and type of emotions (such as excitement, fear, anger, or sadness) in order to produce an appropriate emotional response, to handle emotional over-reactivity, and then to down-regulate to an emotional baseline.

While living on earth awaiting Christ's return and our bodily resurrection with him, there are plenty of reasons for teenagers to get very emotionally reactive—getting extremely angry because of an injustice that happened at school or feeling exceedingly sad because they weren't included in social activities with peers. However, being able to build consistent and appropriate ways to face, understand, and reassess their emotional reactions through godly wisdom and truth is an important area of growth for teenagers. This good work can begin by remembering and returning back to the gospel. Second Corinthians 9:8 says, "And God is able to make all grace abound to you, so that having all sufficiency in all things at all times, you may abound in every good work." It is only this abounding grace—*providing all sufficiency in all things at all times*—that can propel believing teens to good work (i.e., manage their intense emotions). Scripture calls all of us to deal with our emotions, including anger, and be able to manage them because of God's grace through Christ. Ephesians 4:26–27 and 31–32 provides this clear call when one is angry:

> Be angry and do not sin; do not let the sun go down on your anger, and give no opportunity to the devil. . . . Let all bitterness and wrath and anger and clamor and slander be put away from you, along with all malice. Be kind to one another, tenderhearted, forgiving one another, as God in Christ forgave you.

Knowing how teenagers' developing brains and bodies can impact and exacerbate their mental health struggles ought to increase our thoughtfulness, care, compassion, and dependence on Jesus as we interact with them. Similarly, an awareness of teen culture today is helpful to know when caring for struggling teenagers, because it gives us insight into the unique pressures they face as well as ways we can enter into their world.

Teenage Culture Today

Teenagers get a bad rap—they are often seen as mouthy, irreverent, lazy, and impulsive. They certainly can be all those things, but have we ever wondered why? Likewise, sometimes teenagers are stereotyped wrongly and to their detriment. Yet, in our almost thirty years as youth leaders at one church, we have seen these same mouthy, irreverent, lazy, and impulsive teenagers do incredible service for Jesus such as build homes for those in need, construct water tanks in foreign nations facing drought, build orphanages after earthquakes, and repair schools after hurricanes.

We have also raised three teenagers, and in reality, raising teenagers is one of the hardest things we have ever done, and we would say we had relatively "good" kids. Still, we loved them and knew these experiences were part of them growing up. Moreover, as parents who are fallen creatures, our brokenness and sin will cause each and every one of us to experience rifts in our relationships with each other.

The teenage years are also, in many ways, the end of innocence. It's a time of transformation, growth, hormones, and honestly, much difficulty and suffering. These are some of the long-standing characteristics of the teen years that have stayed pretty much the same from generation to generation, although how they are expressed can vary across cultures and times.

Teenagers' developmental stage influences their culture, and the culture in turn also influences teenagers' mental health. What teenagers are experiencing today is different from generations past, and the new challenges they face can feel overwhelming. Let's examine some of the most common pressures currently shaping teenage culture and thereby influencing teenage mental health.

Greater stress

With the weight of social media and the glaring eyes of peers and others always present, even in the privacy of their bedrooms, teenagers face greater stress from expectations, acceptance, success, academics, sports, and social life. They live in a world saturated with social media, which portrays the lives of other teenagers only in terms of their successes. This subsequently leads to them feeling the pressure to also perform well, to look like they have it all together. They experience this pressure not only from the desire to be accepted by their peers, but also to win the approval of their parents, who are experiencing greater pressure to succeed in the eyes of others as well.

Greater violence

Teenagers today live in a society where mass gun violence is prevalent, and weapons can be easily obtained and carried to school. They face bullying and fighting at school. On social media, violence is often glorified, and sometimes it's portrayed in ways that make it seem like a prank, but in fact it poses great danger to teens. Likewise, the violence and danger seen on social media, such as being able to watch school shootings, hear about the dangers of climate change, see the ravages of war, and experience the ups and downs of political instability, are all additional stressors that can impact their mental health.

Increased use of technology

We have personally observed the mental weight associated with students posting pictures of themselves on Instagram or videos on TikTok, or even our youth group posting pictures or videos. Students sometimes became upset when we posted what they perceived as unbecoming or unpleasant pictures of them on social media. They, or their parents, would call us and plead for us to take these pictures or videos down. Teens become envious of other teens' experiences, or feel left out if they are not included, which can lead to anger, disappointment, hurt feelings, insecurities, and even depression or anxiety.

But today, the challenges of technology use are not limited to social media. We have to learn how to navigate a world of smartphones, computers, and video games. As teenagers, how do they learn how to manage the time and involvement they have with these devices? When is it too much? Excessive screen use can even affect a teenager's sleep. Teenagers do not want to get off their smartphones, especially at night. Likewise, their screens can impact their sleep patterns or make it hard for them to fall asleep. Smartphones and electronic screens also emit blue light, which can alter our sleep patterns, making it hard to fall asleep and stay asleep.

But how do caregivers guide and monitor their teens' technology use? Should caregivers even allow social media? On the other hand, what are the costs, such as mistrust and relationship disconnect, if parents look through their phones for detrimental content? At what age do teenagers have a right to privacy? What should caregivers do when their teenager seems addicted to their phones, which causes them to lose sleep or fail to participate in activities? All of these factors and more weigh heavily in the mental health issues of teenagers today.

Sexuality and gender questions

This issue isn't really about dating (although that is also a challenge facing teens today) as much as it is about gender norms and inclusivity. Sexuality and gender questions are some of the most challenging issues in our culture, especially for some teenagers (and their caregivers). While present research indicates only 1.4 percent of teenagers face the clinical diagnosis of gender dysphoria,[8] most teenagers will wrestle with sexuality and gender questions, either through their own struggles or how they should think about and respond to it as Christians. This is an area that can be confusing to both teenagers and their families, and for some, it might also impact their mental health.[9]

Existential crises

An existential crisis involves deep questions about one's purpose in life that cause distress and anxiety. *Who am I? What am I good at? What do I do?* The teenage years are a bridge between childhood and adulthood, and this can be an anxiety-provoking time. Many teenagers also don't even know what they want to do in the future. This has been an issue facing teens for at least a few generations; what is different about this generation of teenagers is that social media has given them a distorted view of how success and accomplishment are defined. The ever-looming questions about the future can feel paralyzing and toxic.

Loneliness and social isolation

Many of us can't hear the words "loneliness and social isolation" without thinking about COVID-19. While the pandemic has certainly been hugely impactful, teenagers have been struggling with loneliness long before March 2020 due to their unique life stage, troubles socializing with peers, and mental health challenges.[10] Loneliness refers to the distressing experience of lacking adequate social connections with others. Ironically, social media might seem to offer more opportunities to connect with others, but in reality it has resulted in more isolation.[11] This has profoundly impacted the mental health of our teenagers today.

A rise in loneliness is also a key factor related to internet use. Recent studies have shown that teenagers in the United States and worldwide increasingly report feeling lonely, even in a period when their internet use has exploded. "They're hanging out with friends, but no friends are there," says Bonnie Nagel, a psychologist at the Oregon Health & Science University.[12] Likewise, she notes, "It's not the same social connectedness we need and not the kind that prevents one from feeling lonely." Often, she says, online social connections amount to seeing "pictures of people hanging out, flaunting it, as if to say, 'Hey, I'm very socially connected,' and 'Hey, look at you by yourself.'"

Increased anxiety

Teens are struggling with anxiety at greater levels than ever. Often, they cannot sleep at night due to their anxiety, and then they are tired at school. Anxious thoughts can focus on issues such as grades and school, who will be their friends, bullying, and pressures from their parents. Anxiety can be a vicious cycle, because unrestful nights and lack of sleep also contribute to it. Anxiety can also lead to a lack of physical wellness and participation in activities, be a barrier to friendships, and incite withdrawal from other positive influences. Anxiety can be brought on by too much time in front of screens and a lack of interaction with others.

Decline in religious participation

Religious participation is declining in America. Moreover, for younger generations, Jean Twenge's research indicates that their participation in religious communities will continue to decrease.[13] This could also mean less participation not only in corporate worship but also in youth ministry. This trend could lead to not only a loss of spiritual community and Christ-centered support systems but also further contribute to the decline of their spiritual, social, and mental well-being.[14]

When I (Danny) was in seminary, I asked a professor about his assessment of the differences and similarities between today's teenagers and those of the past. He answered that due to our human condition as fallen, broken image-bearers of God, living in a broken world, teenagers today are the same as teenagers a generation ago. Theologically, I understood the nuance of what he was saying, but I did not fully agree. Teenagers today are living in their own unique cultural and social context within their developmental stage of life. The impact it has on them is different from both the generations before and the generations that will come after. For this generation in particular, the challenges of this age have greatly impacted their struggles with mental health. Hence, it is important to understand current teenage culture so we can be better equipped to enter into their struggles with the word and hope of the gospel that never changes.

CHAPTER 4

How We Can Help Teens Struggling with Mental Health

In this chapter we will discuss some of the general principles and practices that can guide church leaders and parents in counseling struggling teens in their churches and homes. It is important to be clear that we are not speaking of professional counseling here, although there are certainly times when people with expertise in specific areas of struggle will need to be a part of the care team. That being said, the church is a vital component of caring for teens suffering from mental health challenges.

A pastor or youth leader can often serve as a good initial resource to families, enabling parents to take first steps in supporting a struggling teenager. However, unless they have others in their family who struggle with mental health issues, parents may not initially be comfortable with navigating professional mental health resources, especially if they aren't even sure what is going on. Additionally, sometimes teens with challenging behaviors are not struggling with mental health issues and simply need some spiritual guidance or someone other than their parents whom they can talk to. And even when other resources are needed, the church can continue to provide encouragement and the kind of wisdom that only comes from above (James 3:17).

Evaluate the Situation

As churches and parents, one of the things we need to do is try to distinguish between normal developmental struggles and problems versus mental health struggles. Teenagers in their adolescent years might have issues and strife with their families in different ways, seek freedom from authority, or even act out because they desire independence from the adults in their lives. These kinds of behaviors might just be expressions of typical adolescent struggles versus signs of a mental health issue.

One tool for distinguishing mental health issues from typical teen struggles is to consider if there have been any major changes in the teen's behavior or habits over the past few months, such as shifts in sleeping or eating patterns. Parents might notice their teenager repeatedly staying up late or being really tired in the morning for many days. Likewise, they might notice a drop in their grades in school, a loss of interest in activities they once were passionate about, withdrawal from friends, or even outbursts or unusual changes in their prevailing mood. When possible, it is advisable for parents to stay attuned to their teenagers' social media posts, or discreetly ask their friends or youth leaders about them, to be aware of any shifts in the tone or content of their posts.

The church and youth ministry must also be wise and seek to understand a teenager's struggles in their context. This is so important. A teenager's issues might be biological or hereditary. On the other hand, a teenager's problem might be rooted in a family issue at home. A struggle might also be multidimensional as it could be a combination of biological, psychological, sociocultural, and spiritual. It will be important as a church and youth ministry to consider all these various factors and not just treat a problem solely as a mental health issue.

Err on the side of caution and encourage the family to seek out other perspectives—especially an evaluation from a primary care physician or pediatrician—to determine whether there might be any biological or medical issues going on. If it is discovered that there is a medical issue or serious mental health struggle such as bipolar disorder or schizophrenia that requires professional help, these matters also intersect with the spiritual, so the church should still play a significant role in bringing help and healing to the teenager and their family by walking alongside them through these challenges.

When Possible, Meet with the Family

Because of the complexity of these situations, family meetings or family counseling is always something to consider when possible. When a teenager is struggling with a mental health issue or any other kind of problem, it is often prudent to eventually counsel the family together. We say eventually because sometimes individual help might be sufficient to counsel a teenager in their struggles. Likewise, a family setting for counseling might not always be possible. There might be an issue between the parent and teenagers that needs to be taken care of first, which might have to be dealt with on an individual basis, at least at the beginning. There might be some factors, such as trust issues, that a teenager has with their caregiver that also might need to be worked out before the caregiver can be brought into a counseling situation. But hopefully, if it is a complex or ongoing issue, we can bring help to the whole family context and partner with the parents in bringing about growth and healing for everyone involved.

Show Grace

Showing the love and grace of God will help a teenager know there is no shame in the struggle they are going through, which can be an important way to help them work toward healing. Most teenagers struggling with mental health issues come to church feeling judged, small, or invisible. Helping them see the grace of God through Christ in their sin and suffering can go a long way.

Over the years, one consistent pattern we have seen in those who struggle with their mental health is that they feel like something is uniquely wrong with them and they are "defective"—absolutely flawed. The questions of "What is wrong with me" or "Why am I like this?" are rampant and even painful. We have found it so important to have our church home be a place where struggling teenagers can feel safe and know the grace of God in their suffering. As Isaiah 46:4 states, "Even to your old age I am he, and to gray hairs I will carry you. I have made you, and I will bear you; I will carry and will save." In demonstrating to teenagers that we will not leave them, that we will walk alongside them as they struggle, we show them what the kindness of God is like and they begin to experience relief from their burdens, finding hope that they are his beloved, redeemed by the life, death, and resurrection of Christ on their behalf.

Build the Relationship

Prioritizing and building a strong relationship with a struggling teenager is essential for parents, pastors, and lay leaders. If they don't trust us or feel loved by us, teens will not honestly share what they're going through or be receptive to any help or advice we might try to provide. This is vital for us to keep in mind because caring for teens struggling with mental health will often be difficult, discouraging work. At times we might feel frustrated with them and deem them rebellious or unwilling to help themselves, but through it all we must remember that our relationship with them is a tangible way they can experience the steadfast love of Jesus.

Intriguingly, many studies on both adults and adolescents have found that the *quality* of the counseling relationship itself, apart from the treatment approach (e.g., cognitive behavioral therapy, psychodynamic therapy, person-centered, or eclectic), contributed to positive treatment outcomes.[1] In other words, the strength of our relationship is a significant part of helping teens' mental health improve, aside from any other wisdom or help we provide. This is important for parents to understand, as well as anyone else ministering to teenagers.

But how do we build a strong relationship with a struggling teen? A comprehensive systematic review identified some of the particular qualities and conditions that helped therapists build a strong relationship with their clients.[2] Although a pastoral or parental relationship is different from the counselor-counselee relationship, because of God's common grace we can glean insights from studies such as these to help us grow in building better relationships with struggling teens. And as we filter these insights through the lens of Scripture, we can see that they help us understand the Bible's wisdom for relationships in a deeper way.

The systematic review found that therapists who were able to establish strong relationships with their clients were open and shared reasonable and relatable information about themselves.[3] When we are helping someone, we might think it's our job to only ask them questions and draw them out and then give them advice based on what we hear, but they are much more likely to be vulnerable with us if we are first vulnerable with them. We can show that we are real human beings with a variety of interests, experiences, and struggles of our own. When we share our interests, we might be able to bond as friends by discovering that we have a shared passion for music, sports, or art, for example. Even if we do not discover a common interest, simply sharing what we're passionate about can make us more relatable and help the teen feel comfortable sharing what they care about, the things that are near and dear to their heart.

When we share relatable experiences from our teenage years or struggles that we've gone through as an adult, we help the teen see that we understand to at least some degree what it's like to be a teen and what it feels like to suffer. In doing so, we imitate our incarnate Lord, who took on flesh and sympathizes with our weaknesses, "who in every respect has been tempted as we are, yet without sin" (Hebrews 4:15). Knowing Jesus's sympathy for us is the basis for the exhortation, "Let us then with confidence draw near to the throne of grace, that we may receive mercy and find grace to help in time of need" (Hebrews 4:16). We want to build a sympathetic, understanding atmosphere so that teens feel confident in sharing their burdens with us. Of course, as we share about ourselves, we must guard against oversharing information that is inappropriate to the relationship or making the conversation all about us without intentionally opening up opportunities for the teen to speak. As Proverbs 10:19 warns, "When words are many, transgression is not lacking, but whoever restrains his lips is prudent."

At the same time, while we aim to provide a sympathetic atmosphere and take the youth's distress seriously, the systematic review cautions us against over-validating the thoughts and emotions the teen expresses.[4] A significant part of mental illness is catastrophizing, ruminating, and distorted thinking, so we must be careful to not reinforce their errors even when we are focused on building our relationship. Jeremiah 17:9 tells us that "The heart is deceitful above all things," so we must not fall into the trap of only empathizing with and affirming what the teen says. Showing genuine care, interest, and sympathy does not mean we unconditionally accept everything they do or say. We must be wise and thoughtful about when and how we challenge them, but a strong, compassionate relationship is not antithetical to loving disagreement. There is a time to "weep with those who weep" (Romans 12:15), but we are also called to "admonish the idle, encourage the fainthearted, help the weak, be patient with them all" (1 Thessalonians 5:14) as we noted earlier.

Other important characteristics of therapists who built strong relationships with their clients were their stability and predictability as adults.[5] They were relaxed and calm, able to move back and forth between being formal (authoritative) and informal (friendly). Ephesians 6:4 commands fathers to not "provoke your children to anger" and Colossians 3:21 says, "Fathers, do not provoke your children, lest they become discouraged." While these commands are explicitly directed to fathers, they can warn all of us who take on a parental role of providing guidance and wisdom to our younger brothers and sisters in Christ. There are many ways we can provoke (or "exasperate," as some translations put it) those whom God has placed under our care, but a significant one is being inconsistent or unreliable. If we want teens to trust us, we need to be trustworthy. Additionally, some of the characteristics that the systematic review found got in the way of building a strong relationship included lacking respect; labeling and stigmatizing; being distant, uncaring, or "authoritarian"; and not providing opportunities for the teen to make choices.[6] These are all ways that we can provoke teens to anger and undermine our well-intentioned efforts to help them.

For many of us, these findings from the systematic review are not surprising. They align well with our common sense and with biblical wisdom for relationships. However, we often struggle to remember these things and to believe them enough to put them into practice when our natural instincts, due to personality or sin, tell us to do the opposite. But even when it's hard, we encourage you to grow in putting these principles into practice. In my (Monica's) experience, when I focused on building a strong relationship with the teen I was caring for—when I aimed to be gentle, kind, patient, and humble and wisely consider when and how to press in or pull back by asking questions, reading Bible passages, providing timely biblical instruction, or praying together—they expressed more hope for change.

Feeling the weight of the significance of our relationship as parents, pastors, or youth leaders can become burdensome, but it is lightened when we remember that we and our teens have access to the most powerful relationship of all, the one that brings ultimate healing—our relationship to Christ! God's love has broken the curse of sin and death and has reconciled us to him; as a result, we have already received the most necessary healing of all—the resurrection of our souls from death to life. Now, because of Christ, our God who began a good work in his children will be the one who will "bring it to completion at the day of Jesus Christ" (Philippians 1:6). As those who labor to care for struggling teens, we can rest in knowing that it is God who gives growth. As Paul noted, "I planted, Apollos watered, but God gave the growth" (1 Corinthians 3:6). As we aim to build strong relationships with the teens in our lives, we can rest in the security of our loving relationship with God, who loves our teens far more than we ever could.

Listen Carefully

As soon as we begin to sense that we have some relational trust and have some understanding of their struggles, we might want to begin advising the student. Solid, biblical advice is important. But it is very easy to move too quickly through the listening process. Simply helping them feel heard can be a powerful way to minister to teenagers with mental health issues. Additionally, any advice we offer is much more likely to hit the mark if we've taken the time to actually understand what is going on, and the teen is much more likely to accept our advice if they genuinely believe that we understand them. However, many of us are not as good at listening as we would like to think we are! Listening well and attending to the teenager's suffering involves both non-verbal and verbal expression. To listen well, we need to use visible encouragers, reassurances, restatements, reflection of feelings, and summarizing.[7]

Important encouragers when listening include eye contact, smiling or not smiling as appropriate, nodding, and giving brief verbal expressions of understanding or engagement ("Uh-huh," "Yeah," "Right," "Wow"). These "visible encouragers" help draw out teens and keep them talking when they otherwise might stop. We must be thoughtful about when we use visible encouragers and how much we use them. Overusing them can be just as detrimental as not using them enough! If you're unsure about how you're doing with these, invite someone to observe you having a deep conversation with someone else to give you feedback on the quality and quantity of your visible encouragers.

Reassurances such as "That must have been really hard," "That's really painful," "What a tough situation," "I hear you," "Good job!" and " I've been there too" are ways we can help teenagers to not feel alone, especially if we also share appropriate similar experiences. When they feel reassured, teens will often open up more. We can also further draw out teens by picking up on their nonverbal cues and helping them reflect on their feelings and thoughts. We might say something like, "It can be really uncomfortable talking about this. There is no rush, so take your time." Then you can ask them how they feel and what they are thinking. Here's another example. We might say something like, "I noticed that you looked down when you said . . . . You might be experiencing some tough feelings. Can you tell me about what you are feeling?"

When we restate what teens have said, we help teens feel understood, and we also have the opportunity to make sure that we are understanding them correctly. We can say things like "I hear you saying . . . ," "Can I check to see I have understood you well? It sounds as though . . . ," "Looks like the situation is . . . Am I hearing you accurately?" When we ask for their feedback on our restatements, we are communicating that we truly care about them and want to make sure we have understood them rather than make assumptions about them.

In addition to restating what they have said, we can also summarize what we have heard. Summarizing is similar to restating, but a summary usually aims to tie together general themes or highlights over an entire conversation or series of conversations, whereas restatements are used to check understanding of shorter segments of a conversation. Summarizing can be used to begin or end a conversation, to transition to another topic, and to provide clarity in lengthy, complex stories. For example, we could say, "Last time we talked about . . ." to begin a conversation. To transition we could say, "So, here's what I've learned so far . . ." And at the end of a conversation, we could summarize by saying things like "Today, we looked at . . . ," "Some of the following things seem to stand out . . . ," "First, . . . second, . . . Does that sum it up?"

Another important component of listening carefully is learning how to ask wise questions. Good questions help us to get to know the teenager better. Good questions can communicate interest and care to the teenager (e.g., "It sounds like it's been really hard to stop worrying about all the bad things that might happen next. What do you fear will happen?"). Good questions can motivate a teenager to consider a change or try something out (e.g., "What have you tried before to deal with these thoughts that you are a failure? How did that work for you? Would you be interested in trying something else?"). Good questions can help guide us in discussing that which feels so painful to talk about (e.g., "You are so courageous to be willing to talk about this trauma. When you shared about your trauma before, what things helped you to talk about it? What were unhelpful things you experienced from others? How do you think I can be helpful to you today?"). Remember, however, that you do not want to bombard teenagers with questions in such a way that it sounds like an interrogation. Sometimes, asking too many questions can also promote distrust. Asking multiple questions at one time can be confusing. Pepper your conversation with a mix of open questions (e.g., "Could you tell me about how you felt when that happened to you? How's that affecting you? What's that like for you?") and closed questions (e.g., "What day did that happen? What happened before that incident? What happened afterward?"). Certain kinds of questions reveal certain kinds of information:

- "What" questions can uncover general information.
- "How" questions reveal the way something was done.
- "Why" questions uncover a teenager's purposes, desires, goals, or motivations.
- "How often" and "Where" questions can reveal themes and patterns in a teenager's life.
- "When" questions can reveal the order of events.

Listening and attending well to teenagers is an important way we can love them and help guide the conversation toward the hope of the gospel of Christ in ways that are specific to their experience and struggles. Not only is each mental health issue different, but also each person is different. What might seem like a good help and solution for one student might be different for another. This might seem obvious, but it is vital to be aware of and make sure we are taking the time to really listen to the specific teen in front of us.

I (Danny) have ministered to a few students with eating disorders in the past. What I realized is that for one student, their issue with an eating disorder was more physiological, in that it had to do with their diet and what they were ingesting into their body, which was causing not only a negative reaction in their body but a strong desire not to eat. Two other students with the same eating disorder were struggling with their perceived appearance and their desire to be socially accepted by their peers. However, even though these two students both struggled with their appearance and the desire to be socially accepted, one we were able to help within our church context, and the other needed to find additional help from a mental health professional. So please know that there is not a one-size-fits-all solution for every mental health challenge, which means that we must be prepared to listen carefully and respond flexibly as the situation requires.

Encourage Responsibility

We also want to encourage our teenagers to take responsibility for their lives and not remain in their struggles. As we counsel the teenager, we will most likely begin to identify ways they need to change, and so we will need to consider how to lovingly challenge them to do so. This may take some time to do, and cultivating a relationship first is important to remember. But receiving instruction from their parents and the church is also part of their sanctification.

For our own teenager who struggled with mental health, we knew we had to give him room to rest and recover from all the struggles he was experiencing and to have some important sessions with a counselor. But as time passed, we also knew we needed to lovingly encourage him to work toward facing his mental health in his normal routines of life. The same was true for teenagers in our church. We never came right out of the gate and told them that they needed to "suck it up" and live better lives. However, in time, we did encourage them to grow to resume living normal rhythms of life.

Practice Wise Confidentiality

Although often our goal will be to involve the whole family, we must keep in mind that confidentiality is important in working with teenagers, so how you handle it will go a long way. There have been many times when a teenager in our church has come to us and said they are struggling with a mental health issue. Sometimes, it might not actually be the case, but other times, for example, their stress and anxiety levels have grown so much that it has led to suicidal ideation. When it comes to working with a teenager, navigating confidentiality can be a challenging issue. So, what can be done?

For starters, as a church and youth ministry, we want to build trust with them, so betraying their trust is never helpful. However, there are certain situations where confidentiality must be "broken." In these situations, we let the teenager know that we need to break their confidentiality because it is either legally or ethically warranted, and we strongly urge you to also be transparent with the teens you are caring for when you need to inform others of their situation. For example, as mandated reporters, when a teen has informed us of sexual or physical abuse (either done to them or by them), we let them know that we are required by law to report the incident they shared about. Ethically speaking, when a student might potentially harm themselves or another person, it is important to tell the proper people about the teenager's intentions. Some of these proper people might include the police, a doctor, a mandated reporting call center, and a parent or caregiver. Again, whenever possible, we would advise churches and youth ministries to let the student know first in full transparency, as well as the reason why you are doing it.

More generally speaking, when a situation arises where telling a family member or parent might seem beneficial to the teenager (e.g., when an increasing substance use issue would endanger themselves or others), we generally have provided three options to help and encourage them to share their situation with a parent. This is something a ministry mentor shared with me (Danny) a long time ago. First, we can offer "I will tell them" as an option—I can tell their caregiver or parent about their situation and have a talk with their family on the teenager's behalf. This can sometimes provide a sense of relief for the teenager. Second, we also say, "You can tell them." If they take this option, we give them some time and space to go and share with their caregiver first and let them know we will follow up with their parent or caregiver a few days later. Finally, we also offer "We will tell them." In this option, we arrange a time and place to go together with the teenager to share with their parents the struggle they might be dealing with. Last, in the rare circumstance that a teenager does not want you to share with their caregiver and you know that you have to, in our pastoral and professional experience, it is important to let the teenagers know in full transparency that you really need to inform their parents out of deep care and love. While it might seem like you are breaking some sort of confidentiality, in good faith, you are being honest and transparent with the teenager first.

Cooperate with Civil Authorities

Parents and churches need to know their legal obligations and ethical obligations. Romans 13:1–7 is clear that our general relationship with the government should be submissive obedience to its laws, except when the government forbids what God commands, or commands what God forbids (Exodus 1:15–21; Daniel 3:1–18; Daniel 6:1–10; Acts 5:27–29). This principle also applies to navigating mental health situations in our churches. Over the years, it has been wonderful to have my wife, Monica, as a trained biblical counselor and licensed psychologist for many reasons. One of those was understanding our church's legal obligations—especially regarding mandatory reporting—when a teenager came to us for counseling issues. The law varies somewhat from state to state, so please perform your due diligence and research the requirements in your state, but here are some guiding principles.

First, your church and youth ministry need to know who mandatory reporters are according to your state laws and what obligations they have by law. Generally speaking, mandated reporting laws in each state require that certain individuals are legally obligated to report suspected or known cases of child abuse or neglect to the appropriate authorities. In addition, your church and youth ministry need to understand the steps involved in making a report. Since your youth ministry and church most likely utilize many ministry volunteers, it's important that they also understand the legal authorities they need to report to in cases of suspected child abuse or neglect and the appropriate person within the church they need to notify when a mental health issue is shared with them.

When situations arose where we were not sure about our legal obligations, we found both county and state offices helpful places to call and ask our questions. We had a situation where a middle school student was inappropriately touched by a slightly older male student before she began attending our youth group. Years later, when she was a twelfth grader and the male student had gone off to college, she shared with us about the incident that had happened years before, saying she felt like she was abused sexually. The situation was confusing for me (Danny) to know how to handle, because they were both so young when it happened and it had been four years since the incident. Likewise, the matter was further complicated because the male was now a legal adult. However, when we called the number to potentially report this situation, they answered and clarified all my questions, and what needed to be done became very clear.

Plan for Emergencies

If a teen has expressed suicidal thoughts, they should not be left alone until they have been evaluated and it has been determined that they are not at high risk for suicide. This does not mean the parent must constantly be by their side; they could also be with another trusted adult, such as a ministry volunteer or pastor. Even if the teen has not indicated increased risk of suicide from a suicidal thought, an important safety measure parents should take is to ensure that there are not any easily accessible ways for their teenagers to harm themselves in their homes (e.g., unlocked firearms or strong medications that could cause death if overdosed), should that risk at some point increases. If a teen has self-harmed, we advise the family to go to the local emergency room so that the level of risk of danger can be assessed by a professional. In cases of potential harm to others, we tell parents that they need to call the police. Another resource parents and teens should be aware of is the National Suicide Prevention Lifeline, which is available 24/7 by texting or calling 988 for immediate help. As a youth and family pastor, I (Danny) always let caregivers know that I am available to support them in the event of an emergency to help their teenager or be by their side. Depending on the details of the family's situation and the teen's mental health challenge, there could be other things to consider when planning for safety, but in terms of preserving life, these are some of the most important steps to take. For more information on suicide, see chapter 13.

Keep Pastoral Notes

When a teenager comes to your church or youth ministry to discuss their mental health, it is always prudent to take some notes. However, since you are not an official counseling center, there is a difference between what a professional counselor does and what we might do in a youth ministry or church.

I (Danny) think of my experience with students who were potentially in harm's way, such as cases of self-harm, suicidal ideation, or even abuse. Taking some form of pastoral notes can serve as a safeguard to both the teenager and to the church/youth leader giving help, in case there is any misunderstanding or even if a worst-case scenario event were to happen. I (Danny) recall a few examples over the years of students struggling severely with suicidal ideation. One student I remember even tried to harm himself after youth group when students were hanging out. It was a terrible situation. Ultimately, while all students in these serious cases were eventually referred to a counselor, when they met with me to talk, I also kept some pastoral notes of our meetings.

Find Strengths

In most cases, teens struggling with mental health issues also struggle with questions of identity and worth. The church can help teenagers see their purpose and giftings in the Lord. As Ephesians 2:8–10 says, "For by grace you have been saved through faith. And this is not your own doing; it is the gift of God, not a result of works, so that no one may boast. For we are his workmanship, created in Christ Jesus for good works, which God prepared beforehand, that we should walk in them." By grace we are saved, and through that same grace we are transformed into God's masterpieces. Teenagers need to know that by God's grace they have a great purpose in the Lord's kingdom. Regardless of the nature of their particular struggles, helping them see their identity and purpose in the Lord can be a great encouragement to them.

Opportunities for Care

Mental health issues present great challenges, but they also present rich opportunities for the church and youth ministries to reach out and partner with families and their teenagers. Likewise, for parents of teenagers reading this book, the church can be a wonderful place to find support and help when your teen is struggling with mental health. If these kinds of resources are not readily available in your church, perhaps you could share this book or some of the ideas you've read in it with your church leadership to give them a deeper understanding of how they can help your family.

Ultimately, our desire is that church cultures continue to move away from stigmatizing mental health struggles, and for leaders in the church to be aware that these issues often occur among teens, so we all need to be prepared to help. We can walk alongside teenagers with mental health struggles in a variety of ways, and we hope this chapter provided some of the general principles and practices to keep in mind as we do so. In Part 2 we will discuss specific mental health struggles and ways we can help. However, before we do, we must consider not only how churches can help struggling teens, but also how we can care for their caregivers.

CHAPTER 5

Special Consideration for Caregivers

Teenagers' mental health affects more than just suffering teens themselves. In a 2022 Pew Research Center study on parents' concerns for their children, parents ranked mental health struggles—such as anxiety or depression—as their top concern, above such issues as their teen being bullied, abusing drugs or alcohol, or conceiving a child. The former US Surgeon General Dr. Vivek Murthy recognizes how mental health concerns have become more prevalent in recent years; parents are "not only contending with the usual stressors, but they're also worried about how to manage social media and phones for their kids, something that my parents didn't have to worry about. They're trying to figure out how to contend with a youth mental health crisis and a loneliness epidemic that are hitting kids really hard right now."[1] If you are a parent of a teenager struggling with a mental health issue, part of that struggle will be your own worries, fears, doubts, and deep concerns. As churches, we need to compassionately understand this burden as well and be a place where parents can reach out for help.

No doubt about it—parenting in general is hard. I (Danny) will say it again: raising teenagers is the hardest thing I have ever done—even though my children were relatively good kids. Proverbs 22:6 says, "Train up a child in the way he should go; even when he is old he will not depart from it." This proverb captures the general principle that faithful parenting often bears good fruit in the lives of our children, but something that is important to keep in mind with this verse is that it *is* speaking of the future. While we are in the present, in the midst of actively parenting children in our households, this good work will not be easy. And when our child is undergoing mental health challenges, it will be even harder. Over the years, we have identified some specific practices that can help parents navigate this difficult season. If you are a parent reading this book, we invite you to consider how you could incorporate these ideas into your life. If you are a leader in your church ministering to parents struggling with their teens' mental illness, prayerfully consider how you can encourage them to engage in these helpful practices.

Meditate on Our Gospel Hope

As parents, it is important to remember that more than anything else—more than new parenting strategies, a good night's sleep, medication, a listening ear, or a deeper understanding of mental health—more than all of these good things, we need the hope of the gospel. When we live in light of the gospel, we can show gentleness, compassion, and grace to our teens and to ourselves. Jesus has paid for all of our sins, including our failures as parents and our teens' poor choices; there is nothing any of us has done or will do that can go beyond the reach of Jesus's blood. Although we and our teens may suffer consequences here on earth for our sins or mistakes, we can rest in knowing that in Christ, our eternal destiny is secure. As we muddle our way through confusing and difficult days, we can stay anchored by holding onto God's promises, which always come true. Here are a few promises that can be especially helpful for parents to hold onto as they wrestle with fears for their child and are burdened by feelings of discouragement:

- "And I am sure of this, that he who began a good work in you will bring it to completion at the day of Jesus Christ" (Philippians 1:6).

- "You shall not fear them, for it is the LORD your God who fights for you" (Deuteronomy 3:22).
- "And we know that for those who love God all things work together for good, for those who are called according to his purpose" (Romans 8:28).
- "Come to me, all who labor and are heavy laden, and I will give you rest. Take my yoke upon you, and learn from me, for I am gentle and lowly in heart, and you will find rest for your souls. For my yoke is easy, and my burden is light" (Matthew 11:28–30).
- "'For the mountains may depart and the hills be removed, but my steadfast love shall not depart from you, and my covenant of peace shall not be removed," says the LORD, who has compassion on you" (Isaiah 54:10).
- "If any of you lacks wisdom, let him ask God, who gives generously to all without reproach, and it will be given him" (James 1:5).

These are rich promises that can be a source of comfort to any of us going through difficult times, but also don't be surprised if these particular promises don't bring comfort. Sometimes when a verse is very familiar, or applied in unhelpful ways, it doesn't speak to the heart. This is why it's important to stay immersed in reading Scripture regularly, hearing the preaching of God's Word, and studying the Bible in midweek small groups or Sunday school. The "word of God is living and active, sharper than any two-edged sword" (Hebrews 4:12), but we can never be entirely sure about which passage will be the one that God will use to pierce our hearts or bring comfort to our souls. We can be sure, however, that consistent, receptive immersion in God's Word will produce good fruit—it will not return to God empty, but will accomplish the purpose for which he sent it (Isaiah 55:11).

Keep Lines of Communication Open

When teens are struggling with mental health issues, sometimes parents are afraid to talk to them because they're worried that they'll say the wrong thing. This is a legitimate fear; there certainly are unhelpful things we can say to someone struggling with mental illness. However, not saying anything at all is usually worse. We need to not be afraid to start conversations with our teens, especially if we notice anything potentially strange or unusual in their behavior lately. This is difficult to do, so please don't be discouraged if this describes you as a parent.

A good practice is to establish some kind of regular check-in time with your teen. We are not talking about a daily check-in, which might come across as suffocating or anxious. We often tell parents at our church to remember to "be the parent." By this, we mean that our calling as parents is to model God to our children, who is *bigger*, *stronger*, and *wiser* than they are and is undeservedly *kind* to them. We want to be a compassionate and dependable presence in their lives, so as much as possible our aim should be to shield our children from carrying the burden of our fears for them in addition to the burden of their other struggles.

So, what could a helpful check-in look like? It begins with identifying a regular time, perhaps on a weekly or biweekly basis, where you can have each other's undivided attention. If you haven't had a consistent check-in time with your teen in the past, be upfront with them that this might feel awkward at first, but make it clear that you are doing this because you love them and want to prioritize intentional time with them. Tell them you are sorry that you have not always done this consistently in the past. You do not need to mention that you're implementing this new practice because you're worried about their mental health. Instead, this should be a space where they can just share and talk about their lives more generally, and hopefully as they grow more comfortable with the process and you ask good questions, they will also begin to open up about their mental health struggle. But even if they don't, this can be a time of repairing past hurts and ensuring that they know you love them and care about the details of their life.

Of course, there will be times when your teenager doesn't feel up to it. When that happens, you can just express your love for them and say, "We can do this another day, but this time is important, so let's look at our calendars to see when we can reschedule." And as you experience the awkwardness of the first few times and encounter resistance, be patient.

To ease into this, you might even simply hang out in their room—linger a little bit more each time—even if they don't say anything to you. I (Monica) did this when my sons were teenagers. First it started out with popping my head through their closed door and simply asking them, "How's it going?" When they became used to that, I hung out on their bed, lingering a little more each time while they were doing their own thing. Then at some point, they began to share, and we would have good conversations. It will take time to build this rhythm with your teenager. If you need ideas for what to discuss during this time, you can try some of the exercises in Part 2 of this book.

Additionally, keeping lines of communication open is where the church and youth ministry can be of big help. Sometimes due to the developmental changes teens are going through or because of past family conflicts, they stop being willing to open up to their parents. However, they may be more willing to talk to another significant adult in their lives, such as a pastor or youth leader. Once the teen has opened up to a trusted adult about their struggles, they often find it easier to also share what they're going through with their caregivers, either on their own or in a family counseling context. Parents, please know that your teenagers not being willing to talk to you is often normal behavior for adolescents, but you can still keep lines of communication open by seeking out other adults who they might be more willing to speak with.

Traditionally, most youth ministries have aimed for a 5:1 ratio of teens to adults, especially for mission trips or retreats. Years ago, Chap Clark of Fuller Seminary proposed that churches reverse this ratio and seek to have five significant adults for every one student.[2] Even if they're not going through a mental health challenge, teens need adults who care about them and know them well. Although finding five adults willing to build a relationship with each teen in our church might sound impossible, if we are creative and persistent I believe we can find them; many people want to serve others in the church, but they simply don't know how to do so. Some people we should consider are youth ministry leaders or volunteers, small group leaders or Sunday school teachers, older grandparent-like figures, or even a mature young adult the teen might look up to as someone just a little further ahead in life, but still close enough in age to remember what it's like to be a teen. Regardless of what this ends up looking like at your church or for your teen, the heart of the matter is that parents, churches, and youth ministries need to proactively consider how to keep lines of communication open for teenagers.

Establish Daily Rhythms

Dealing with the mental health struggles of teenagers can definitely be an up-and-down experience that changes daily, with good days and bad days. In the midst of this turbulence, committing to daily healthy rhythms can provide some stability and help with maintaining health during a stressful season, both for parents and teenagers. Some daily rhythms to consider are proper sleep, spending some time in prayer and reading God's Word, and having dinner with your teen (daily, if possible, but at least a few times a week). This can also include physical exercise like a daily walk or working out a few days a week. From raising teenagers ourselves, we know they are busy, but if they are busy because they are hanging out with friends, going to church youth group, or participating in other social activities that they enjoy, having a structured schedule can be helpful for their mental health. However, take care that a busy schedule does not turn into a chaotic schedule that gets in the way of establishing healthy life rhythms for yourself and for your teenager.

Parents (and youth leaders) often ask us how parents can help their teens establish healthy daily rhythms, particularly if they are resistant. How can they encourage their students to go to bed earlier, eat dinner with the family without their cell phone, or perhaps even just talk with their parents? What we believe is the most important and most practical first step is what we noted earlier in the book—we tell parents to remember to live out their calling as parents and to model God to our children, who is *bigger*, *stronger*, and *wiser* than they are and is undeservedly *kind* to them. Again, we want to be a compassionate and dependable presence in their lives. So, in the case of our teenager being resistant or even rebellious to us in establishing rhythms in their lives, as much as possible, we must model God to them. That means not reacting in anger or exasperating them, but instead showing grace and compassion, laying out clear guidelines and expectations in love, and enforcing appropriate consequences when necessary—understanding also that our teenagers might disobey and fail.

Reach Out for Help

Proverbs 11:14 reminds us "Where there is no guidance, a people falls, but in an abundance of counselors there is safety." This verse encourages us as a body of Christ to see how the counsel of others can provide great help and aid. As parents, opening up about our children's struggles with others in the church won't always be easy. Hopefully, your church is equipped to provide refuge and guidance for you, or they are at least willing to grow in their awareness of and care for teens struggling with their mental health. As Proverbs 11:14 suggests, there is great "safety" for us in getting the help of others, and our churches can be that for us as parents. The church is the body of Christ, and 1 Corinthians 12:12–26 tells us that we are called to care for all parts of the body. Reach out to your pastor or your teen's youth leader. Share not only about your teenager's struggles, but also about your own struggles.

Not only can we reach out to our pastors, but it can also be incredibly helpful to reach out to a friend. 1 Thessalonians 5:11 says, "Therefore encourage one another and build one another up, just as you are doing." While it might be difficult, we encourage you as a parent to reach out to a friend in your difficulties, even if you fear being judged or misunderstood. Even though it can make us feel very vulnerable to share about mental health problems in our families, having a friend walk alongside us in this journey can be a great encouragement and help. The advice they offer can help us see our situation from a different perspective, but even more importantly, our friends can pray with and for us throughout this challenging time, however long it may last.

When one of our sons had his mental health struggles, we tried different things to help him, such as working with the school counselor and school psychologist, asking his youth pastor for help, and seeking help outside of both school and church from a counselor. Eventually, this counselor suggested that we come in as a family for counseling. Granted, not every teenager wants this, and in our experience, we have seen some teenagers reject this possibility with their counselor. Other times, parents have suggested themselves to see a counselor in a family setting. There is sometimes a need for this when a teenager is having a mental health issue. This does not necessarily mean a parent or caregiver is at fault for or the cause of the teenager's mental health struggle; it just means that addressing the relationship dynamics in the family can be an important part of providing holistic care. In our case, we were able to talk about the present struggles and situations our teenager was facing, as well as find out more definitively about the bullying our teenager had experienced a few years before in school that had impacted his mental health. We even talked about his childhood and how I (Danny) sometimes fueled his past and even present anxiety struggles. It was eye-opening and difficult at times, but very helpful in so many ways.

Consider the Power of the Tongue

As parents, sometimes it seems as though our teens have no interest in what we have to say and are completely tuning us out. However, they are listening even when they don't seem to be, and our words have more power than we realize. James 3:1–12 tells us that although the tongue seems a small thing, it can have an outsize impact, just as a small rudder steers a whole ship, or a whole forest is set ablaze by a small fire. When our son was struggling with his mental health, Monica introduced me to the concept of expressed emotion (EE), which is a measure of how family members spontaneously talk about or react to those with a mental illness in unhelpful ways, such as critical comments, hostility, and emotional overinvolvement. Studies have shown that a high level of EE in the home can worsen the prognosis for patients with mental illness (such as schizophrenia, depression, bipolar, or eating disorders).[3]

Monica introduced the concept of EE to me because it was hard for me to comprehend my son's anxiety or empathize with it, which slowly turned to frustration as he continued to struggle with it. In loving parents, examples of EE can often be subtle and not seem overtly critical or hostile to the parent expressing the sentiment:

- "Stop being anxious."
- "If they would only overcome/understand . . ."
- "If my kid would only be aware of . . . , they could fix it."

- “What’s wrong with my kid?”
- “When will you get over this?”

The frustration behind these comments can, if not addressed, lead the caregiver to try to find quick or easy solutions that backfire and instead create further negative emotions and disappointments for themselves and their teenager, creating a vicious cycle. High levels of negative emotions expressed also undermine our teens’ trust in us and security in our love. This, in turn, also makes them less likely to share what’s really going on in their hearts and less receptive to any advice or help we try to offer.

If we recognize that we have negative emotions expressed toward our teens’ mental health struggles, this is a situation where it can be very helpful to pursue family counseling or individual counseling for ourselves. Although as loving parents it is right and good for us to be deeply concerned about our teens’ mental health struggles, it is also important that we focus on what’s within our sphere of control—our own words and actions. We must be seriously pursuing our own growth in godliness. Ephesians 4:29 tells us that our aim as mature Christians is to “Let no corrupting talk come out of your mouths, but only such as is good for building up, as fits the occasion, that it may give grace to those who hear.” Let us pray fervently to God: “Set a guard, O Lord, over my mouth; keep watch over the door of my lips” (Psalm 141:3). The book of Proverbs is full of helpful verses to meditate on as we learn how to bridle our tongues (including Proverbs 10:19; 12:18; 15:1–2; 15:4; 15:28; 17:27–28; 18:6–7; 18:21; and 21:23). Choose one that strikes you deeply and meditate on it day and night so that the next time you are tempted to speak rashly, you can recall the words you have hidden in your heart and pray to God for help so that your words would build up your teen and give them grace (Ephesians 4:29).

In addition to learning how to control our tongues, we should also pursue deep heart change so that the underlying attitudes behind our words are addressed. Jesus taught us that "it is not what goes into the mouth that defiles a person, but what comes out of the mouth; this defiles a person" (Matthew 15:11). This is because the words of our mouths reveal our hearts: "For out of the abundance of the heart the mouth speaks" (Matthew 12:34). What do our critical, hostile, and impatient words reveal about our hearts? We may be surprised to discover the roots of these thoughts and emotions. Exploring these things with a pastor, counselor, or close friend can help us pursue the deeper, heart-level change that is pleasing in God's sight and will be far more helpful to our teens than if we only seek to grow in controlling our tongues (although that is incredibly important too, since there will always be sin and foolishness in our hearts that can slip into our words if we are not careful).

In this heart-level change, thanks be to God that it will not be about doing more and more or becoming masters of our own sin more and more, but it will be again and again about how we will be swallowed up or mastered by the abounding grace of God through Christ. Then through the assurance and comfort that comes with the gospel of Jesus Christ, we will be compelled to grow in godliness. Growing in this gospel-saturated godliness will enable us, as parents, to be stable sources of gentleness, peace, and love to our teens in the midst of their turmoil. Like Jesus, we will be able to not break the bruised reed or quench the faintly burning wick that is our teenagers (Isaiah 42:4).

Develop a Care Plan

Hopefully your church or a counselor can help you with this, but if not, it's important to take the time to develop a care plan for your teen and yourself. The first thing to do is to know who to reach out to in case of an emergency. In terms of physical danger, whether harm to self or harm to others, calling 911 for police or medical support is of course an important go-to resource. Additionally, be mentally prepared to take your teen to the emergency department if there has been harm to self, or call the National Suicide Prevention Lifeline, which you can reach 24/7 by texting or calling 988 for immediate help if your teen has expressed suicidal urges or intent. But aside from physical support, consider who you can reach out to for spiritual and emotional support, both for yourself and your teen. Is there a pastor or elder in your church who you can reach out to in an emergency? A close friend? If you have other children at home, who can you call on for help to care for them while you are caring for your teen in crisis? Asking these individuals ahead of time if they would be willing to help you in an emergency can help you feel loved and supported and help emergency situations feel less stressful so that you aren't left scrambling to figure out who to ask for help in a tense and precarious situation.

In addition to planning for emergencies, a good care plan will also identify the who, what, when, where, and how of bringing others in to support you and your teen. This could look like having a weekly phone call check-in with a friend or pastor, regularly inviting others into your home or getting together for coffee, setting up counseling appointments, lining up practical help for things like running errands, housecleaning, meal chains, and childcare or fun experiences for siblings in the home (who are also affected by the stress and instability of having a sibling with a mental health struggle, and are often receiving less attention from their parents). As parents we may feel reluctant to ask our churches and friends for help in these ways because we are ashamed of being a "burden" to others, or because we think we can "handle it," but even if we are fully capable of handling meals, housecleaning, and such, it can be more helpful than we realize to have some of these other tasks taken off our plates so we can devote more time to praying, receiving counseling, or loving and spending intentional time with our dear children. We all have a limited amount of time available, so if we need to spend more time caring for a struggling child, where will that time come from?

Our brothers and sisters in Christ cannot replace us as parents, but they can cook a meal or clean our home so we can be more available to parent our child.

Ultimately, whether you are a parent needing help and support or a church or ministry leader wanting to offer support to parents, it is important to remember that Galatians 6:2 calls believers to "bear one another's burdens." This includes not only helping a teen struggling with mental illness, but it also means coming alongside the whole family and helping everyone impacted. First Corinthians 12:26 says, "If one member suffers, all suffer together; if one member is honored, all rejoice together." This is true not only in the church as a body, but also in the family unit. We are all connected to one another and affected by one another, so we must prayerfully consider how we can be a blessing and bear one another's burdens.

CHAPTER 6

When Is a Situation Beyond the Church's Scope?

In Romans 12:3, Paul writes, "For by the grace given to me I say to everyone among you not to think of himself more highly than he ought to think, but to think with sober judgment, each according to the measure of faith that God has assigned." Ministry leaders seeking to help teens and their parents will need great humility and sobriety in judgment, as well as tender care and love for them. Parents surely desire this kind of careful, humble assessment from their church leaders, but we must also approach our churches with humility. In this chapter we will consider how we, parents and church leaders, walk in humility together to assess when there is a need to look for help outside the church.

Key Considerations

When and how do you determine that a mental health issue is beyond the church's scope? Ideally, answering this question will involve conversations between pastors and parents, but in some situations pastors or parents may need to make this call on their own. Over the course of our ministry, we have had countless conversations with teens in various settings that were, in one form or another, spiritual counseling. But we also experienced situations where there were mental health issues that would benefit from specific expertise that we could not offer as a church. As we have thought through these issues, we have identified some key considerations that have guided our decision-making. We offer these questions here in the hope that they will help you think carefully about the situations you are facing as a pastor or youth leader, or as a parent if your teen is struggling with a mental health issue.

What is best for the teenager?

Mental health struggles often have multiple and complex emotional, spiritual, relational, psychological, and physiological layers. As a church, we can certainly offer spiritual wisdom and counsel to a teenager who, for example, seems addicted to computer games, or a student who is feeling lonely and rejected by her friends. However, the more layers involved and the deeper the layers go, the more likely it is that they will need more comprehensive help and specific expertise. Sometimes as pastors or youth leaders, our own egos might get in the way of admitting that; we want to help, and we might think we know what is best for a student and their family. However, we must always keep at the forefront of our minds that we need to recommend what is best for the teen, not what will make us feel more successful or significant. For parents, you may desire the situation to be handled solely by the church for various reasons, but if that is not what is best for your teen, are you willing to let go of that desire? It's not always easy to see what is best for each teen, but we must at least remember that *is* the primary goal, not any other considerations that we might subconsciously allow to take precedence.

What do my instincts tell me?

In a 1964 Supreme Court case on obscenity law, Supreme Court Justice Potter Stewart coined the phrase "I'll know it when I see it." As a youth pastor for twenty-nine years, I (Danny) could often instinctively see that the issue a teenager was struggling with was more complex. A teenager crying every time she talks about her anxiety or a student who is so stressed that he did not want to go to school for days often needed more than just the church's help. I remember many years back we had a student who came to church and youth group weekly who suddenly took a strange turn. He would come to youth group and just stare at the ground. This happened for a few weeks. At first we brushed it off as unusual; he wasn't being disruptive to his small group or acting out. Then, after a few weeks, he would not only stare at the ground, but he would also murmur words to himself, which eventually turned into what seemed like groaning. As this went on for a few more weeks, his groaning started getting louder and became frightening to others in the youth group. It had become more than just a little strange. At that point, his small group leader knew something was wrong and so did we. This student definitely needed some professional mental health help that was beyond the scope of what we could offer as a church.

Sometimes parents will come to a pastor indicating a desire to find a mental health professional outside the church because they intuitively sense that something deeper is going on. Parents, if this is your desire, let your pastor know when speaking with them, and they may be able to help you think through these decisions. Although our instincts can be wrong, many times we can pick up on warning signs that we can't quite articulate, but we know that something is off, particularly when we know the person well and we know what they're normally like. Additionally, do not discount the work of the Holy Spirit in leading you to desire to explore various possibilities, and at least have the peace of mind knowing that you did all you could to provide the best care possible for your child.

Are there liability issues?

It is important to consider liability issues for your church when it comes to the care of a teenager and their mental health struggles. Your church and youth ministry do not want to be in over their heads and be negligent or mistreat a teenager in their struggles. This could open up you or your church to liability issues, in addition to potentially causing real harm. Your church must consider this and proceed with caution. Be careful about making definitive statements about whether a person does or does not have a mental illness, and do not apply diagnostic labels in your care for them. They may come to you self-diagnosing or with a diagnosis from a qualified mental health professional. In that case, you will benefit from knowing about that diagnostic category and taking in this information along with all of the other information you glean from talking to and observing them, but avoid giving them or their parents the impression that you have diagnosed them with or are "treating" them for anxiety, depression, or the like. Of course, feeling anxious or depressed are also common words used to describe the human experience, so you don't need to go out of your way to avoid using these terms, but do be thoughtful about how you use them and particularly about using diagnostic terms such as ADHD, bipolar disorder, PTSD, and such. If you establish a formal counseling relationship with a teen, be sure to have the teen and their guardian complete paperwork indicating that they are seeing you for spiritual advice and counsel, not medical advice.

Depending on your church's theology, you may be more or less prone to see demonic possession or oppression. Even if you have good reason to suspect demonic involvement, do not assume that is the only thing going on. Aside from any liability issues, it would be terrible to discourage someone from receiving the proper care they need because you erroneously concluded that they were demon possessed or oppressed. Err on the side of caution and get outside help; you can still continue to pray for them and minister to them as they receive medical or mental health care. Even if that care is ineffective because the teen's issues are primarily due to demonic activity, at least you will have done your part in helping parents rule out those possibilities.

Parents, consider that not obtaining medical or mental health treatment for your teen could be neglectful. It could potentially be a real risk, particularly if your teen is showing significant, physiological signs of distress or is posing a risk to harm themselves or others and you are not taking reasonable steps to safeguard their own or others' safety. We do not wish to frighten you into immediately taking your teen to see a mental health professional at the slightest sign of mental disturbance, but do be aware that this is a risk you are taking if your teen is significantly struggling and you choose to not pursue professional help.

Am I at risk for burnout?

Sometimes in church ministry, we may be equipped in terms of training and experience to help a teen with their particular struggle, but due to staffing issues and the needs of other people in the church we may find that we need to outsource care to others to avoid overwork and the burnout that usually ensues. You may notice in your church that one teenager or family is consuming an enormous amount of time and energy. This is understandable during an acute crisis, but as time goes on this is not a sustainable situation. While we want to care for them, there are limitations we all have, and sometimes the best course of action, both for them and for the church as a whole, is that they seek professional help. That is not to say we do not care for them or are not attentive to them, but we will need to put boundaries around how much time we can spend on helping them and the kinds of help we can offer them. Outsourcing care to other organizations or individuals does not mean that the church completely ceases their involvement.

As parents, we need to understand the limitations that our churches might have, and that if your pastors recommend that you reach out to others for care for your teen, whether inside or outside the church, this does not mean that your family is unimportant to them, or that they are shirking their duty to shepherd your family. Burnout is also a significant risk for parents when their teen is struggling with mental health issues. Bringing in professional help can provide real relief, as well as reaching out to brothers and sisters in

Christ for support in other practical ways (see chapter 5 for specific ideas).

Is there risk of harm to self or others?

There are mental health situations that could be potentially harmful for the person suffering from it. In cases of severe depression, for example, if a person discusses suicidal thoughts and behaviors, we tell caregivers to go to the emergency room right away. If a teen girl is dangerously thin and malnourished due to an eating disorder, this can be life-threatening and requires expert help as soon as possible. On the other hand, they could be a potential danger to people around them, such as their caregivers, their siblings, or people at school. If we have any concerns about them hurting another person, we should get help. This might include informing the parents, school officials, or local authorities such as the police. These situations usually present themselves when a teenager discusses hurting others or perhaps acquires a weapon.

Is the situation interfering with daily life functions or growing worse?

Sometimes we notice a teenager who had been attending youth group suddenly stops coming or has a very different demeanor or pattern of interaction at church. Or parents might share that their teen is doing poorly in school, seems tired all the time, is regularly getting into fights at home or at school, or is exhibiting strange eating patterns or other odd behaviors. Anytime a teen's behavior begins to significantly impact their ability to engage in daily life tasks such as eating, sleeping, socializing, or fulfilling school or work responsibilities, we strongly consider the possibility that they would benefit from seeing a professional counselor.

Sometimes, a teenager's or family's circumstances change as you are providing care to them. Things could get worse, or the nature of the problem changes. Or, as you provide care, you might discover that there are much deeper issues going on than were apparent at first. In these cases, be willing to admit that your care alone is not sufficient for their needs; pridefully continuing when your counsel is not helping or is insufficient is dangerous and not in the teen's best interest.

Are there signs of a physiological issue?

Over time, you may begin to suspect a teenager's problems stem from a medical or biological situation that are beyond your abilities. This is often the case with illnesses like schizophrenia, tumors that impact brain functioning, neurodevelopmental disorders such as autism, and some sleep or eating disorders. In these cases, we know that the medical or biological situation is beyond our expertise as a church, so we definitely need to suggest other means for a family to get help. Again, this does not mean that the church stops ministering to the teen or family, but we will not seek to be the primary source of care in these situations.

Has there been abuse or other significant trauma?

Child abuse is a profoundly difficult topic to discuss fully here. However, we recommend *The Child Safeguarding Policy Guide for Churches and Ministries* by Basyle Tchividjian and Shira M. Berkovits[1] for a way to develop policies and procedures to protect children and teens and deal with possible child abuse.

In terms of loving wisely and well, an important thing for the church and youth ministry to do, is develop proper plans and procedures for safeguarding teens from child abuse. This could include requiring mandated reporter training for all adult volunteers and youth workers. While not all states require youth ministry volunteers to undergo a training on recognizing and reporting child abuse, this would be a way to practically love teenagers well. As we discussed in chapter 4, the specifics of who are considered mandated reporters and how their reports should be made varies from state to state, so each church will need to do their own research on this, but it is imperative that you do so if you haven't already. In addition to complying with all mandated reporting laws in your state, it is essential that teens who have experienced abuse or have abused others receive additional care from people with training in abuse. Pastors can and should continue to minister to them as well, but child abuse is a complex issue that can impact many different areas of life.

Additionally, pastors and church leaders should be alert to signs of post-traumatic stress disorder (PTSD), which can arise due to a variety of severe traumas, including car accidents, witnessing interpersonal violence, abuse, rape, near-death experiences, traumatic childbirth, or being diagnosed with a life-threatening illness (for more information on PTSD, see chapter 12). If a teen under your care has undergone a severe trauma, they should receive mental health care. Pastors and youth leaders can certainly counsel teenagers through how they are interpreting the trauma they've experienced and how they are relating to God after their trauma, but these are often significant issues that also benefit from professional expertise.

Additionally, signs of PTSD can occur long after the traumatic event. A few years ago, we had a teen in our youth group who was mild-mannered and quiet but consistent in her attendance, so we developed a close relationship with her. During one of the meals that we shared with her after school, she told a troubling story of an experience she had when she was much younger at what seemed like a cult-like organization posing as a church. She recounted experiences of leaders bombastically "praying" over her and her siblings, calling upon them loudly to repent, and saying that they had demonic spirits in them. This seemed to have happened over a period of a few years when she was in elementary school. Well, we didn't dig into this story too much, yet we comforted her and tried to help her process it. But it did not end there.

Because of the pain of those years and experiences, she began to text us late one night. She "rage" texted, sending fifteen to twenty texts in a row, rapid fire. She started texting how she "cursed out God," how "ashamed she felt," how "she messed up big time," how she felt like she was "going to go to hell," and that she felt terrorized by God. Finally, she said she felt like she was going insane. From these texts, we knew things were not normal, and the fact that she had a very traumatizing experience was now revealing itself in some serious episodes that impacted her mental health. We immediately called her parents, rushed over to her home after they expressed needing more support, and proceeded to help the parents take this teenager to the emergency room. From there, she was admitted into an inpatient mental health center. Over time, she received solid care and was discharged. After being discharged, we reached out to her and were able to reconnect with this teenager pastorally, as well as helping her reconnect to the youth group even as she continued to receive outpatient treatment. The parents expressed their thankfulness as they also felt pastorally cared for. This teenager later began to ask deep questions about faith, so we helped her through that journey as she grew in her walk with God. In time, she even became a student leader in our youth group, all the while working through PTSD. Ultimately, it is important for pastors, youth leaders, and parents to not overlook signs of PTSD, even if they are unaware of significant trauma or if the trauma occurred a long time ago.

When Teens or Families Resist Going to Counseling

For pastors and youth leaders, there most likely will be situations in your church where you think through the questions we described in the previous section and you decide that it would be in the teen's best interest to receive care from a mental health professional. However, you should be prepared to receive resistance to this idea, either from the teen, their parents, or both. Knowing possible sources of this resistance can help you consider how to best respond. Parents, if you recognize that you resist the idea of receiving mental health support from someone outside of your church due to one of the following reasons, discuss this openly with your pastor and they may be able to help you work through the issue.

Cost or logistics

Mental health care is often not cheap. In fact, it can be very expensive. One of the things we can do as churches is to help families and their teenagers find ways to offset costs. Many places that offer counseling services might have some sort of financial aid, depending on your income. Helping parents know about these options and how to apply for them can be a significant way to overcome this issue. Other types of mental health care might be covered by insurance, but many parents are unaware of this or unsure about what kind of mental health coverage their insurance offers. In our church, we also have a deacon's fund, where the cost for a certain number of counseling sessions can be either fully or partially covered. It took some work on our part to make mental health service costs an allowed use of the deacon fund and to develop parameters around its use. If you have established procedures for offsetting the costs of mental health care, make sure your church members know about this so that cost does not have to be a barrier to receiving care.

Some families may struggle with the logistics of receiving mental health care, either alone or in addition to struggling with the cost. Perhaps the only available appointment is at a time when neither parent is available, or the family only has one vehicle or no vehicle at all, so transportation logistics are a significant barrier. If you discover that issues with time or transportation are a barrier to the teen receiving mental health support, see if there are ways someone in your church can help the family overcome these issues. Many parents may be embarrassed to admit that they are limited in these ways, so you may have to directly ask if they need transportation assistance for their teen's appointments.

Availability

Many counseling organizations and mental health care providers are severely limited in their availability for new clients. Many geographic regions do not have adequate levels of mental health care providers for their population. As a result, there are often long wait times for people seeking professional mental health care. The church and youth ministry should be aware of this and help families and their teenagers in both searching for the proper mental health care as well as providing care and support while they wait for an appointment slot to open. We are not saying that the church and youth ministry attempt to offer mental health care in the meantime, but we can offer pastoral care and solace for families and teenagers until availability opens up. Parents, if you are unable to access the mental health support your family needs in a timely manner, make sure your pastors are aware of this so they can provide your family with additional support while you are waiting.

Embarrassment

There are times when a family or teenager might resist going to counseling or mental health services because they feel embarrassed, and they may even get angry if you suggest it. This has sometimes happened to us; in different cultural contexts, there can be greater or less shame and stigma associated with mental illness, so it is important to be aware of your context and sensitively shepherd teens and their caregivers through the process of realizing and accepting their need for mental health services. Be prepared to carefully ask questions to identify the roots of their embarrassment and do what you can to address those concerns with Scripture and rationales that they will find compelling. And be patient; this may take a great deal of time. As a parent, if you recognize that you don't want your teen to go to counseling outside of the church due to embarrassment, be open about that with your pastors and be willing to listen to their responses to your thoughts and feelings. If your teen is resistant to going to counseling and you realize it's because he's embarrassed, discuss that with your teen and bring others whose opinion they respect into the conversation as appropriate.

Fear or ignorance

For some families and their teenagers, there might be great fear about getting mental health care, which often can be rooted in ignorance. It could be that they fear being deemed "crazy" or believe that only really "lunatic" people get mental health treatment. They might not understand what happens in a counseling session. They might fear being "labeled." They might not know the basic differences between a counselor, psychologist, and psychiatrist. If you suggest going to a non-Christian mental health professional, parents may fear that their teen's faith will be undermined by the counseling they receive. Our churches and youth ministries can help assuage some of these concerns by offering to go to the first appointments with our families and teenagers. You most likely will not be let into the appointment itself. But as a form of care and shepherding, being with a family and teenager might relieve some of their fears, and you can help them debrief the experience afterward. Parents, if this is you or your teen, do not be afraid to ask for help and a pastoral presence from your church.

Humility, Sober Judgment, and Faith

Ultimately, considering whether a mental health situation is outside the scope of the church requires the humility, sober judgment, and faith described in Romans 12:3. It will take all three of these elements for all involved, whether you are a parent or church leader. At times we will make mistakes and have lapses in judgment, but our hope is that by prayerfully thinking through and discussing these questions, parents and churches will have greater clarity on when they might need to involve people with more expertise in mental health issues. As we faithfully pursue wisdom in these difficult situations, we can rest in knowing that God is faithful and good, and he will provide for our needs (Philippians 4:19).

Part 2

Caring for Teenagers with Specific Mental Health Struggles

CHAPTER 7

Teenagers with Anxiety and Stress

Audrey was generally pleasant, but sometimes she could be moody. Her parents noticed that a few weeks ago, Audrey had started becoming more irritable and impatient with them and her brother. However, they were not concerned. Audrey was still responsible and very motivated—she completed her schoolwork on time, was active with her friends, and participated at school and church youth events.

As the weeks passed, Audrey began to complain more and more about how much schoolwork she had and how she really needed to do well. Her parents also noticed that she would more frequently become angry over seemingly small issues that she hadn't gotten angry about in the past. Audrey's parents heard her complaints about school and tried to tell her that kind of stress is hard, but normal. In addition, they tried to address her anger and her negative attitude as a Christian. They would sometimes wonder and worry, "If she can't handle this stress now, how is she going to handle it when she has to take care of more things?" They would also think that if she had more faith in God, she would not complain this much or have this kind of anger and irritability. They wondered if they needed to simply be patient with her moods and hope this was a phase that she would get over, or if they needed to get her more help as well.

One day, Audrey woke up feeling unwell and asked her parents if she could stay home from school. When her parents asked about her sickness, she said she felt nauseated and tired, had a bad headache, and had not slept well. Her parents asked about her plans to catch up on schoolwork. Audrey responded that she could go back to school tomorrow and follow up about missed work with her teachers or friends. Over time, Audrey began to more frequently ask to stay home because she felt ill; as she missed more school, her grades began to drop. Without her parents' knowledge, Audrey began using e-cigarettes. Eventually, as Audrey's parents became more and more concerned about her attitudes and behavior, they sought help for her from their church.

Audrey's story is just one example of what anxiety might look like, but there are many other ways in which teenagers experience unmanageable anxiety. Although there are other anxiety conditions that many teenagers deal with, such as panic attacks and social anxiety, we will focus this chapter on the more general form of anxiety. This type of anxiety is excessive and uncontrollable worry over daily situations that produces a significant amount of distress for the teenager, making it difficult for them to do everyday activities, such as being around friends, going to school, and keeping up with schoolwork or other tasks. Along with excessive and uncontrollable fear, teenagers with anxiety can feel on edge, get easily fatigued, and experience restlessness, difficulty concentrating, muscle tension, and sleep issues.

While the description of generalized anxiety in the DSM (*Diagnostic and Statistical Manual of Mental Disorders*) does not differentiate between how an adult or teenager experiences it, studies show that teenagers, unlike children and adults, show elevated emotion processing center (i.e., amygdala) activity to cues of potential threat.[1] As mentioned in chapter 2, this heightened emotional activity along with immature connections between the cognitive control center and the motivational-emotional areas of the brain result in an imbalance in managing fear/anxiousness. This imbalance may lead to heightened emotionality and sensitivity to experiences of threat, leading to susceptibility to anxiety issues.[2]

One of the largest studies done on teenagers found that anxiety disorders affect 32 percent of teenagers between ages thirteen and eighteen years old, and anxiety conditions affect girls more than boys at a rate of 2:1.[3] Some of the risk factors for anxiety disorders include shy or behavioral inhibited traits; a parent with an anxiety disorder; anxious, critical, and overprotective parenting styles; and trauma.[4] Although some anxiety symptoms may decrease on their own over time, not all do, so it is important to address the condition early on.[5]

Sometimes, in an effort to reduce their anxiety, teenagers might use various counterproductive methods. To escape anxious feelings, teenagers might start to play more video games or engage in other activities that consistently distract them from their distress. They may even experiment with using substances like nicotine, alcohol, or marijuana to bring some quick relief. If their anxiety is left unchecked, teens are prone to developing unhelpful ways to cope with their anxiety, but it does not have to be this way; there are wise and godly ways to respond to feelings of anxiety rather than dismissing, ignoring, escaping, or consistently distracting oneself. Some of the activities and habits described later in this chapter can help you guide teens in identifying more godly ways of responding to and managing their anxiety.

While the significant changes that are happening in teenagers' bodies and brains might make them more susceptible to anxiety amid the stress, it does not mean that they will all develop an enduring anxiety condition. Also, some strong anxious reactions are protective and helpful, like when there is a real threatening situation that requires our bodies to quickly fight, flight, or even freeze. God made our bodies in such marvelous ways to protect us—even in this fallen world. Still, by being aware of this sensitivity, parents, pastors, and youth leaders can show more care and compassion when teenagers' heightened reactivity, emotionality and sensitivity are expressed. Rather than dismissing or ignoring it as simply a stage that they just need to get through, it can become an opportunity to help teenagers press into the powerful hope we have in the gospel of Christ.

The Gospel Amid Anxiety: The Kingdom of God Is Here

Anxiety in this world is nothing new, surprising, or unique, yet it can be very hard to deal with. We will all get anxious from time to time. And the Bible is not silent on our experience of it. In Matthew 6:25–34, Jesus addresses anxiety directly; he cares about the anxiety people experience—their worries about future things. In his Sermon on the Mount, Jesus proclaims that the kingdom of God has arrived, and it is the kingdom of God that can truly break through and address the fears that fuel anxiety:

> Therefore I tell you, do not be anxious about your life, what you will eat or what you will drink, nor about your body, what you will put on. Is not life more than food, and the body more than clothing? Look at the birds of the air: they neither sow nor reap nor gather into barns, and yet your heavenly Father feeds them. Are you not of more value than they? And which of you by being anxious can add a single hour to his span of life? And why are you anxious about clothing? Consider the lilies of the field, how they grow: they neither toil nor spin, yet I tell you, even Solomon in all his glory was not arrayed like one of these. But if God so clothes the grass of the field, which today is alive and tomorrow is thrown into the oven, will he not much more clothe you, O you of little faith? Therefore do not be anxious, saying, "What shall we eat?" or "What shall we drink?" or "What shall we wear?" For the Gentiles seek after all these things, and your heavenly Father knows that you need them all. But seek first the kingdom of God and his righteousness, and all these things will be added to you. Therefore do not be anxious about tomorrow, for tomorrow will be anxious for itself. Sufficient for the day is its own trouble. (Matthew 6:25–34)

In this world, how can teenagers *not* worry about what feels most important in their lives? How can they *not* worry about school and their future welfare, about their reputation and how they look, or about their friendships and family relationships? Yet, because of Jesus, the kingdom of God has broken through into this place where anxieties abound. Because of Jesus, believing teenagers are living in the kingdom of God now, even as they await Jesus's return. Today, amid their anxieties, they can seek first the kingdom of God and his righteousness.

This means that we prioritize living out the implications of the salvation we have been given in Jesus—in the kingdom of God, we can simply focus on loving him and loving our neighbors. The kingdom of God is not as complicated as the demands placed on us by the world! What a comfort it is to know that we need not focus on our reputation or our own success, for Jesus said that our heavenly Father knows about and cares for our needs. And when we do worry again, because we will, we can return to remembering the work of Jesus who reconciled us to God.

Jesus told us in Matthew 6:25 not to be anxious about our lives, but it seems especially difficult for teenagers who have severe anxiety to obey this call. As we care for them, it is important that we not use passages such as Matthew 6:25–34 to condemn them for feeling anxious, but instead as a way to invite them to grow in their trust in him and to cast their cares on him, for he cares for them (1 Peter 5:7). Although we believe that Jesus has already conquered sin and death, brought the kingdom of God to earth, and sent the Holy Spirit to dwell in us, until Jesus returns and everything is made new, we can continue to grow in having his peace that surpasses all understanding (Philippians 4:7). It is not an automatic, once-and-for-all gift given to us upon conversion.

I (Monica) am reminded of a teenager whose severe anxiety got in the way of completing some basic tasks or activities of life. As we worked on addressing her anxiety, she expressed how she was now able to challenge her anxiety when it told her, "You can't have comfort and peace now . . . not until you get to heaven" and instead hold on to the truth that because Jesus is with her now, she can have comfort and peace in the moment . . . *now.* As she continued to press into these promises of God through Jesus again and again in everyday "small" moments, struggling with her anxiety helped her grow deeper in her faith.

Providing Compassionate Care for Anxious Teens

Those who care for anxious teenagers ought first to lean into the assurance, comfort, and rest found in God's completed work on the cross through Christ so they can be a calming presence. When we personally lean into this gospel comfort, we can care more compassionately for the anxious teenager. We need not be distant or demanding since we trust in God's care for his people's needs. Remembering the gospel of Christ will help us to stay present with anxious teenagers and enable us to provide "a good word" in wise and focused ways; as Proverbs 12:25 says, "Anxiety in a man's heart weighs him down, but a good word makes him glad."

In this journey toward peace and away from anxiety, we are guided by 2 Corinthians 10:4–5, which tells us that "the weapons of our warfare are not of the flesh but have divine power to destroy strongholds. We destroy arguments and every lofty opinion raised against the knowledge of God, and *take every thought captive to obey Christ.*" Learning how to take every thought captive is a journey that lasts a lifetime. Our hope is that the practical activities in this chapter can be used to help teenagers learn how to take their thoughts captive when their minds, emotions, and physical body become overwhelmed by anxiety, so that they might know God's comfort and develop a deeper understanding of the God who knows their anxious thoughts before even they do. It is important to note that we only recommend using these activities *after* you have built a strong relationship with the teen and listened carefully to deeply understand the nature of their specific struggle with anxiety (for advice on how to do this effectively, see chapter 4, especially the sections on building relationships and listening carefully). Once you have done this foundational work, you can use your wisdom to select an exercise that can be helpful to them in specific ways.

Riding the waves of emotions[6]

Emotions will come and go. For many teenagers struggling with anxiety, feelings of worry, nervousness, and fear can seem like they don't subside. When big feelings come, encourage the teenager to find a way to move toward calm. After spending some time listening and understanding the teenager with their anxiety and worries that overwhelm, you might say something like this:

> I can see that while there are so many things that are stressful, you are trying really hard not to be anxious or worry, but that's really difficult to do. How you are feeling really matters.
>
> In Matthew 8, Jesus calmed the wind and the waves; if he can calm the wind and the waves, he can bring calm to your anxiety and worry. Will you try this exercise with me?
>
> Although you've tried to get rid of your anxious feelings, they don't seem to go away. You feel on edge, but it's important to know that Jesus doesn't simply say, "Don't be anxious." He says, "Don't be anxious" because of who he is . . . he is the son of God who reigns over every fiber of your being and every part of this world. He is with you.

Then show the teenager the image of the waves:

Notice your emotions.
Your emotions will come and go . . . even the tough ones.
Imagine them like a high wave, coming and going.
Ride the waves of your emotions.
Don't ignore them.
Don't try to hold onto them or make them bigger.
If Jesus calmed the wind and the sea,
he could calm the crashing waves of your emotions.

What sort of man is this, that even winds and sea obey him? – Matthew 8:27

Look at this image of the waves. Notice your emotions; notice your anxiety; notice how you feel on edge. (Pause)

Your emotions will come and go . . . even the tough ones. Imagine them like a high wave, coming and going. (Pause)

Now ride the waves of your emotions. Don't ignore them. Don't try to hold onto them or make them bigger, but notice them. (Pause)

> If Jesus calmed the wind and the sea, he can calm the crashing waves of your emotions.
>
> Philippians 4:13 says that you can do all things through Jesus who strengthens you.

After completing this exercise, ask them how it was for them. Some teens may struggle with wondering why Jesus doesn't immediately calm the waves of their emotions, or with guilt if they fail to calm their emotions since Philippians 4:13 says that Jesus has provided them with the strength to do it. If they voice those concerns, talk them through the theological questions they have and find other activities that help. However, for many teens this exercise can encourage them to notice what they are feeling as an outside observer (and not be completely caught up in the feelings) and submit their feelings to the lordship of Christ, trusting in his power to calm the waves. If they find it helpful, advise and encourage them to do this daily when they feel anxious or on edge. Have them take a picture of the graphic.

Guided breathing

Anxiety not only affects our emotions and our thoughts, but it also affects our physical body. Anxious teenagers may feel tension in various areas of their bodies, like the back of the neck, shoulders, stomach, and other parts. They may also start to feel their heart rate increase and the palms of their hands start to sweat. Breathing exercises can slow down the heart rate to help signal to the brain and body that there is no threat and bring feelings of calm. When teenagers are gripped by anxiety, their sympathetic nervous system (SNS) may be activated and working overtime. The SNS is also known as the fight/flight part of the autonomic nervous system. When the SNS system is activated, the parasympathetic nervous system (PNS) is deactivated. The PNS is also known as the rest and digest part of the nervous system. Deep breathing can slow down their heart rate and in effect, deactivate the fight/flight system and activate the rest and digest system. This ability to deactivate the fight/flight response through a breathing exercise can be an important skill for teens to learn that can be helpful in the variety of stressful situations they will encounter throughout their lives.

However, as believers, we know that it is not just deep breathing that brings true comfort and calm. Rather, true peace comes through faith in the promises and presence of God through Christ and the work of the Holy Spirit. So, while we do encourage use of guided breathing exercises as a way to physiologically calm anxious bodies that impact the minds, it is not a tool we recommend on its own, because it does not deal with the heart issues that are often behind the anxiety.

The 4-7-8 breathing method is one type of exercise that we have found helpful. To do the breathing exercise, have the teenager sit in a comfortable position and then instruct them to slowly take a deep breath in through their nose for four counts, then hold their breath for seven counts, and then slowly breathe out through their mouth with pursed lips for eight counts. Doing this exercise with them can be helpful so that they don't feel strange or alone. You can do several cycles of this breathing exercise. Here is an example of a script you can use:

> Let's now start this breathing exercise. As we begin this exercise together, softly close your eyes. Remember that our God says in Psalm 46, that he is our refuge and strength, a very present help in trouble. And because he is our refuge and strength, he gives you a way for your body to be calmed.
>
> Take a deep breath in through your nose for 4 counts . . . noticing your stomach expand. Now hold it for 7 counts . . . 4 . . . 5 . . . 6 . . . 7. And now slowly breathe out through your pursed lips for 8 counts . . . feeling your stomach contract . . . 7 . . . 8.

> Let's do this again. Breathe in through your nose . . . 3 . . . 4. Hold it . . . 2 . . . 3 . . . 4 . . . 5 . . . 6 . . . 7. Breathe out through your mouth slowly . . . noticing your shoulders dropping and relaxing . . . 7 . . . 8.
>
> Breathe in . . . 2 . . . 3 . . . 4. Hold it . . . 2 . . . 3 . . . 4 . . . 5 . . . 6 . . . 7. Breathe out slowly . . . 2 . . . 3 . . . 4 . . . 5 . . . 6 . . . 7 . . . 8.
>
> Last one . . . breathe in . . . 2 . . . 3 . . . 4. Hold it . . . 2 . . . 3 . . . 4 . . . 5 . . . 6 . . . 7. Breathe out slowly . . . allowing your arms to loosen up . . . 5 . . . 6 . . . 7 . . . 8.
>
> Now you can open your eyes.

When doing this exercise together, if you think it might be helpful, you can have the teenager use a subjective scale to identify their distress level before the exercise, and then after the exercise once it is completed. By using this scale, the teenager can see how much they were able to reduce their anxious distress. Here's how you can ask them to scale their distress level:

> Before we begin the breathing exercise together, I'd like you to tell me how distressed you are on a scale of zero to ten—where zero equals no distress at all and ten equals extreme distress. Take a moment to reflect, then tell me your number.

After completing the breathing exercise, ask them to measure their distress level again using the scale.

> Now that we've completed the breathing exercise, take a moment again to reflect on your level of distress. On that scale of zero to ten—where zero equals no distress at all and ten equals extreme distress—tell me what your number is.

After completing the exercise, have them reflect and discuss how this exercise went for them. If you used the subjective distress scale, talk about any changes they noticed. Encourage them to practice this whenever they experience muscle tensions and feel on edge. Encourage them that after some deep breathing, it can be helpful to meditate on Scripture or pray. Remind believing teenagers that whatever they do, even when they do this breathing exercise, they can "do everything in the name of the Lord Jesus, giving thanks to God the Father through him" (Colossians 3:17).

Writing thoughts and feelings on leaves floating to Jesus[7]

Before a counseling session or intentional conversation, print the "Thoughts and Feelings on Leaves in a River Floating to Jesus" worksheet or the "Thoughts and Feelings: Crying Out to God" worksheet. Many teens struggle with how difficult it is to stop worrying once their anxious thoughts begin. You can introduce this exercise after having an intentional conversation about their anxiety-provoking circumstances, experiences, reactions, and thoughts as a way to help teens learn how to give their anxious thoughts and feelings to Jesus. Ask them to take time to be silent and allow their worries and anxious feelings to enter their minds. Then instruct them to write those thoughts and feelings down on the leaves or the clouds printed on the paper and imagine them moving away from them, floating down the river or up into the sky to Jesus—the One who knows them so well. Ask them to imagine watching each of them floating away.

After completing the exercise, remind them that the Bible says, "Humble yourselves, therefore, under the mighty hand of God so that at the proper time he may exalt you, casting all your anxieties on him, because he cares for you" (1 Peter 5:6–7) or that "Even before a word is on my tongue, behold, O Lord, you know it altogether" (Psalm 139:4). Also, reflect and discuss together how this experience was for them.

Name: ______________________________ Date: ______________

Thoughts and Feelings on Leaves in a River Floating to Jesus

Then the angel showed me the river of the water of life, bright as crystal, flowing from the throne of God and of the Lamb. (Revelation 22:1)

Name: ______________________ Date: ______________

Thoughts and Feelings: Crying Out to God

Even before a word is on my tongue, behold, O LORD, you know it altogether. (Psalm 139:4)

Five senses 5-4-3-2-1 exercise

In Mathew 6:25–34, Jesus addresses anxiety by directing the people's gaze to the birds of the air and the lilies of the field. He tells the worriers that the birds are fed and the lilies are clothed by their heavenly Father. Then he encourages the people to have faith because "if God so clothes the grass of the field, which today is alive and tomorrow is thrown into the oven, will he not much more clothe you, O you of little faith?" (Matthew 6:30).

Jesus invited those who worried to join him in that moment to look at the birds and the flowers. He appealed to their reasoning and guided worriers to notice how the heavenly Father knows their needs and is providing for all of creation, including them, today.

The "Five Senses 5-4-3-2-1 Exercise" can be used to guide teenagers who are having intense anxiety reactions, like feeling jittery or tense or having trouble concentrating, to stay present with Jesus, who is with them now and cares for their needs today. The exercise asks them to do the following:

> Name 5 things in the room that God created that you can see. (Pause)
>
> Name 4 things that God created that you can touch and take a moment to describe what you feel when you touch these items. (Pause)
>
> Name 3 things that God created that you can hear. (Pause)
>
> Name 2 things God created that you can smell. (Pause)
>
> Now this one might be a little tricky, but describe one thing you can taste in your mouth. (Pause)

After the exercise, ask them how they think they did with this and how they felt. When we are anxious, we often become stuck in an internal loop of worried thoughts. Noticing God's creation around us can help us come out of that loop and remember where we are and who is with us.

Taking care of today: kingdom of God living activity[8]

Tolerating feelings of uncertainty by leaning into the certainty of the kingdom of God can be hard for anyone to do, but for teenagers with anxiety, it's even harder. We can use this exercise to discuss and help the teenager to narrow down what they *can* do to take care of today only, when they are having trouble organizing or prioritizing their activities or responsibilities. Many with anxiety think in terms of what they *should* be doing.

In Matthew 6:27, Jesus reminds us of the futility of our anxious thoughts when he asks, "And which of you by being anxious can add a single hour to his span of life?" Instead, he encourages us by going on to say,

> But seek first the kingdom of God and his righteousness, and all these things will be added to you. Therefore do not be anxious about tomorrow, for tomorrow will be anxious for itself. Sufficient for the day is its own trouble. (Matthew 6:33–34)

In the "Taking Care of Today: Kingdom of God Living Activity," we ask teens to write in two concentric circles. In the larger, outer circle we encourage teens to externalize their fears by writing out the things that can be left for tomorrow—things that they may need to do in the future, but that they can do nothing about today. Then, in the inner circle we have them write out the things that they can actually do today. In doing so, we help them limit their thoughts to the things that are within their control that they can act on today, rather than the paralyzing fears for the future that they can't do anything about. In so doing, they can grow in learning how to "seek first the kingdom of God and his righteousness" (Matthew 6:33).

Name: ______________________________ Date: ______________

Taking Care of Today: Kingdom of God Living

Therefore do not be anxious about tomorrow, for tomorrow will be anxious for itself. Sufficient for the day is its own trouble. (Matthew 6:34)

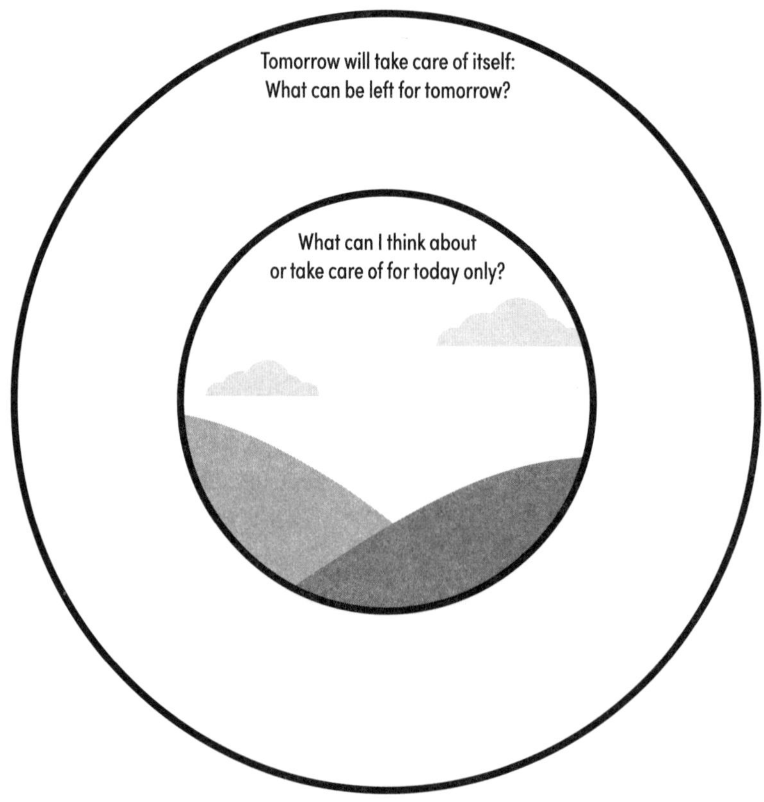

The Benefits of Good Habits

While as Christians we understand that the greatest hope and healing for anxiety comes from the gospel, we also know that as embodied souls, teenagers struggling with anxiety also benefit from receiving other good gifts of God. We know that "Every good gift and every perfect gift is from above, coming down from the Father of lights, with whom there is no variation or shadow due to change" (James 1:17). Studies show that getting regular exercise can help prevent anxiety and depression. People who are more active tend to have fewer symptoms and better overall mental health.[9] Furthermore, maintaining good sleep habits and spending time with positive quality friends also helps with anxiety.[10] In addition, healthy eating habits as well as wise use of social media will be helpful to reduce teen anxiety. Studies show that maintaining good eating habits (e.g., eating fruits and vegetables or having a meal as a family) was found to be linked to better adolescent psychological well-being, while drinking sugary drinks was associated with anxiety and poorer psychological well-being, particularly in teen boys.[11] For specific ways as to how parents, pastors, and leaders can help teens develop wiser uses of social media, see chapter 14. As we point teens to Christ through our conversations and help them develop better ways of responding to their anxiety with these activities, let us not forget to also have conversations with them about their daily habits and how those might be supporting or undermining their mental health.

Warning Signs for When Additional Help Is Needed

If a teen in your care has been experiencing anxiety that has not improved after having intentional conversations for about three or four months, helping them receive more intentional support and enlarging their circle of care would be loving and wise. Here are some warning signs for when additional help is needed even after caring for them:

- Unremitting worries and fears about everyday situations even after the anxiety-provoking situation has resolved
- Still having difficulty staying focused on tasks or conversations
- Still having constant physical symptoms like muscle tension, heart palpitations, jitteriness, headaches, and stomachaches
- Having trouble sleeping
- Avoiding or canceling daily activities/responsibilities or social situations they used to enjoy or are involved in
- Signs of self-harming behaviors like cutting or hitting themselves

Sometimes, while keeping these warning signs in mind, it might still be hard to gauge how severely the teenager might be struggling. Along with identifying these warning signs for when additional help might be needed, parents, pastors, and leaders can use a very simple questionnaire to check for the teenager's level of severity of anxiety. This is a helpful tool that does not require any training to use. This anxiety questionnaire (see figure below) is a publicly accessible short questionnaire for anxiety developed by Drs. Robert L. Spitzer, Janet B. W. Williams, Kurt Kroenke, and colleagues.[12] This questionnaire can be used for teenagers to identify the intensity of a teenager's struggle with anxiety.

The questionnaire is made up of seven questions that ask the teenager to reflect on their experiences of anxiety over the past two weeks. You can either ask the questions to the teenager or you can make a copy of the questionnaire and have the teenager complete it. Each question asks the teenager to identify a number on a scale of zero (not at all) to three (nearly every day). Once the questionnaire is completed, calculate the total score. If the score is ten or higher, that could indicate that enlarging the circle of care can be wise and more help is needed.

Figure 2: Anxiety Questionnaire

During the past two weeks, how often have you been bothered by the following problems?

	Not at all	Several days	More than half the days	Nearly every day
1. Feeling nervous, anxious, or on edge?	0	1	2	3
2. Not being able to stop or control worrying?	0	1	2	3
3. Worring too much about different things?	0	1	2	3
4. Trouble relaxing?	0	1	2	3
5. Being so restless that it is hard to sit still?	0	1	2	3
6. Becoming easily annoyed or irritable?	0	1	2	3
7. Feeling afraid as if something awful might happen?	0	1	2	3
Total Score: ______ = Add columns:		______ +	______ +	______

(Source: Developed by Drs. Robert L. Spitzer, Janet B. W. Williams, Kurt Kroenke, and colleagues; no permission required)

If you are a parent, this increased circle of care and support might involve going to your pediatrician to talk about your teen's anxiety and hearing their thoughts or recommendations. It might involve reaching out to schoolteachers, school counselors, or school psychologists to see how they can be supportive for your anxious teen while they are at school. It might mean helping them receive formal counseling from a mental health professional for their anxiety.

Living in the Kingdom of God

As parents, pastors, and youth leaders who love teenagers and are near to them, we are called to help anxious teens by remembering that we too are today living in the kingdom of God. Because we are living in his kingdom, we are also called to put down our worries, even our worries about how to help a teen who is struggling with worry. While anxiety is a hardship that many teenagers will grapple with and we may feel at a loss about how to help them, because of the gospel, we can remember that God is near us and delights in giving wisdom to all who ask (James 1:5).

CHAPTER 8

Teenagers with Depression

When the stay-at-home orders were given after COVID–19 began, Benjamin felt a sense of relief about not having to go to school. He welcomed the break. But after a few months of staying at home, Ben began to feel bored and irritable, especially since he couldn't see his friends. Attending school through video meetings was starting to feel like a drag. His parents' pressure to keep up with school was increasingly bothering him. Ben began staying up late at night scrolling through social media when his parents went to bed. Months and months passed like this.

When COVID–19 restrictions were lifted, Ben was excited to be able to go back to school, but once school began, he quickly started to feel even more irritable and angry. He started to drop out of activities he used to really enjoy, like band and basketball. After many arguments with his parents, Ben began to drop out of more school clubs. He even began to miss school due to overwhelming fatigue and frequently stayed home from youth group and church. Ben's church friends reached out to share their concerns and to show that they cared about his absence. Even though Ben did not have any suicidal intentions or plans, he wished he could disappear somehow; he felt hopeless and worthless.

Ben was depressed. He was experiencing what is known as major depressive disorder (MDD), which causes significant distress that interferes with normal function at school, work, or social situations. Symptoms of depression can include the following:

- A depressed or irritable mood (could show up as anger)[1]
- A marked loss of interest or pleasure in most or all activities
- A significant change in weight, such as losing or gaining more than 5 percent of body weight in a month, or significant decrease or increase in appetite, or not making expected weight gains for teenagers
- Difficulty sleeping or feeling excessively sleepy during the day despite having adequate time to sleep
- Visibly noticeable restlessness or being slowed down
- Fatigue or loss of energy
- Excessive feelings of worthlessness or excessive guilt
- Difficulty thinking or concentrating
- Recurrent thoughts of death or suicide, or a suicide attempt

In younger children, signs of depression often appear as anxiety, various fears, or phobias, and may be accompanied by physical issues such as stomachaches or headaches. Despite these challenges, they typically continue to engage in activities, perform well at school, and enjoy time with peers. However, as they approach preadolescence (ages eight to twelve), they may start to withdraw from social interactions. By the teenage years, depressive symptoms can closely resemble those seen in adults, with a stronger emphasis on feelings of guilt and hopelessness. However, unlike adults, teenagers will exhibit more behavioral problems. Notable behavioral changes—like angry outbursts, a decline in academic performance, loss of friendships or starting to hang out with a different crowd, and a lack of interest in activities they once enjoyed—can indicate more severe depression. Also, teenagers are more likely to experience disruptions in sleep and appetite and may even have serious suicidal thoughts and behaviors.

The prevalence rates for MDD among adolescents vary, with recent years showing an upward trend.[2] Current estimates of teenagers diagnosed with depression suggest a prevalence of 8.4 percent.[3] This prevalence rate could be higher. According to the National Survey on Drug Use and Health (NSDUH) that collected data from the general population, approximately 20 percent of adolescents in 2021 reported having had a major depressive episode.[4] While the gender ratio is roughly equal in childhood depression, it shifts to about twice as many teen girls who will struggle with depression than teen boys. Some possible factors contributing to the rising rates of depression during adolescence include brain/hormonal changes, increased social expectations, and greater exposure to negative life events.[5]

Although we have a general understanding of the symptoms of depression, there is still a lack of consensus about what causes depression. As Christians, we understand that depression and other severe mental health conditions are ultimately caused by the curse of sin after the fall revealed in Genesis. Because of the curse of sin, many facets of humanity and creation are impacted. It is not surprising when some studies show various dimensions that contribute to depression (e.g., genetics, parental depression, or individual temperament). For example, family and twin studies found that depression can be inherited.[6] Also, regarding the impact of parental depression in a child's developmental environment, longitudinal studies have shown that children of depressed parents face increased risks for anxiety disorders, major depression, and substance abuse, with these challenges becoming more evident in late adolescence, particularly among girls.[7] The graph below illustrates the age-specific rates of MDD over twenty years in children of depressed versus nondepressed parents from the study by Weissman et al.[8] Given these studies on effects of parental depression on children's mental health, if you are a parent who struggles with depression, it would be wise and loving to address your own struggle with depression as you support and care for your teen.

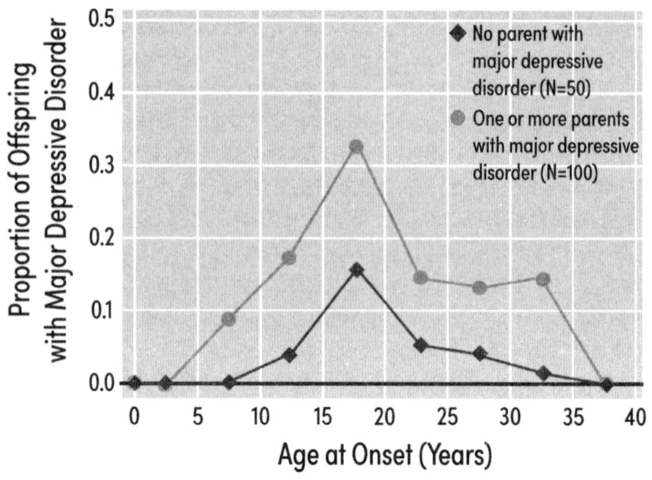

Figure 3: Age-specific Rates of MDD Over 20 Years in Children of Depressed and Nondepressed Parents

During the sensitive adolescent stage, which is also known as the "storm and stress" period, caring compassionately for teenagers means acknowledging that they will be experiencing their emotions more acutely. While they are still growing and developing, they may have greater temptations to make impulsive decisions, especially while depressed. So, it is kind, caring, and compassionate to listen well, acknowledge their experiences, and help them not feel alone. Because we trust that God is with us, even amid an acute experience of mental health issues such as depression, we can focus on reasonable and practical ways to come alongside teens in this struggle and reduce its impact.

The Gospel Amid Depression: Hope in God

When I (Monica) was a teenager, around the age of eighteen, I didn't know it at the time, but I experienced a tough period of severe depression. During that time as a teenager, life felt impossibly heavy, and I often felt like I was dragging myself around. I frequently wondered, "Why is everything so hard?" I was a very good student in high school and received several top merit awards, but once I started college, I just couldn't make myself go to my classes. As a commuter, I would drive to the university, park my car, and sleep there until I had to either go to work or go home. I felt numb, disconnected, confused, ashamed, lacked motivation, and felt utterly hopeless. While I suffered, I desperately clung to God and cried out to him while trying hard to remember the greater hope I had in Christ. Although I did not think about killing myself, I did often ask God to bring an end to all of this and longed to be with him sooner than later. I remember often saying to Jesus, "Come, Lord Jesus, come!" while in distress.

The psalmist's description in Psalm 46 of the earth giving way and the mountains being moved into the heart of the sea describes my experience of depression as a teenager—all of life felt like it was falling apart and there was nothing good. Even though I did not feel it or fully understand it, as Psalm 46 also says, God was my refuge and strength, my very present help in a time of trouble, even in the midst of depression. During that time, seeing glimpses of hope in God amid the intractable depression enabled me to put one step in front of the other. Psalm 42:11 shows the necessity of placing our hope in God as a pathway out of depression—"Why are you cast down, O my soul, and why are you in turmoil within me? Hope in God; for I shall again praise him, my salvation and my God." Hoping in God that I would one day feel better and praise him again meant that I could be depressed *and* get up in the morning and keep driving to school. Hoping in God that I would one day feel better and praise him again meant that I could be depressed *and* still dream—building my imagination for a purposeful future.

Bringing the hope of God to bear upon the lives of depressed teenagers is a significant way to minister to them. Depressed teenagers feel tired and weary, beaten down by their minds and moods while dealing with depression alone. However, our God has not left the depressed teenager alone. He cares compassionately for the tired, exhausted, and weary teenager, and there are numerous Scripture passages that can shine the light of hope into the darkness of depression.

Isaiah 40:1 starts with "Comfort, comfort my people, says your God." This is a message of comfort for exhausted, tired, and weary teenagers battling depression. Our mighty and everlasting God does not grow tired and weary even when they have. As Isaiah 40:28–31 says,

> Do you not know?
>   Have you not heard?
> The LORD is the everlasting God,
>   the Creator of the ends of the earth.
> He will not grow tired or weary,
>   and his understanding no one can fathom.
> He gives strength to the weary
>   and increases the power of the weak.
> Even youths grow tired and weary,
>   and young men stumble and fall;
> but those who hope in the LORD
>   will renew their strength.
> They will soar on wings like eagles;
>   they will run and not grow weary,
>   they will walk and not be faint. (NIV)

When we feel weary and weak, these words might seem to describe an impossibility—how could I ever soar on wings like eagles, run and not grow weary, or walk and not be faint when just getting out of bed feels like an insurmountable hurdle? However, because these words are a promise from God, we can trust that someday they will come true. One of the features of depression is the belief that the situation is permanent, that it will never change. But as we learn how to hope in the Lord, our strength will be renewed. It may not be today, or tomorrow, or even months from now, but the day will come when we will experience the renewing strength of the Lord, whose strength never fails. This is the kind of truth that a depressed heart needs to hear and meditate on day and night.

As for me, even though I was not aware that I was depressed when I was a teenager, I incessantly clung to God's truths and promises in Jesus, of his plans for peace and a future. One of my favorite passages I read repeatedly and memorized was Hebrews 12:1–2—looking to Jesus:

> Therefore, since we are surrounded by so great a cloud of witnesses, let us also lay aside every weight, and sin which clings so closely, and let us run with endurance the race that is set before us, looking to Jesus, the founder and perfecter of our faith, who for the joy that was set before him endured the cross, despising the shame, and is seated at the right hand of the throne of God.

Knowing that Jesus despised the shame of the cross and overcame death on my behalf, I felt emboldened to make small changes in my behaviors, while yet feeling my shame, guilt, and weight of depression. One small step I took was in going to at least one class rather than sleeping in my car. By making changes to some of these behaviors, it cut short the feelings of shame and guilt that had locked me into an unbearable feedback loop. I was then able to take one more step. Then I took another step and another. The ultimate lifting of depression took several years for me—thanks be to God! But I can imagine that it could have been even better if someone were to draw near and walk alongside me. So, parents, pastors, and youth leaders, drawing near and being with teenagers who are struggling with depression is valuable, loving, and so kind.

Providing Compassionate Care: Drawing Near and Being With

We believe that Jesus has conquered sin and death, ushered in the kingdom of God, and given us the Holy Spirit; however, until Jesus returns again, believing teenagers will still struggle with depression. The darkness of depression can weigh down on the hope we have in Christ that one day everything will be better. As sojourners, we and struggling teenagers must be reminded of 1 Corinthians 2:16, which says, "'For who has understood the mind of the Lord so as to instruct him?' But we have the mind of Christ."

In this section are practical activities that a parent, pastor, or leader can use to help teenagers take their depressed thoughts captive and experience the hope that they have in God, who knows them intimately and cares for their hardship. Our desire is that these activities not only bring hope to alleviate teens' depression, but also help them trust in the saving grace of God, take to heart his promises, and grow more intimate in their relationship with Jesus. Our hard times are opportunities for discipleship and sanctification. It is important to note that we only recommend using these activities *after* you have built a strong relationship with the teen and listened carefully to deeply understand the nature of their specific struggle with depression (for advice on how to do this effectively, see chapter 4, especially the sections on building relationships and listening carefully). Once you have done this foundational work, you can use your wisdom to select an exercise that can be helpful to them in specific ways.

Writing thoughts and feelings on leaves floating to Jesus[9]

An important tool for teenagers to help manage or deal with their depression is to practice crying out to God with their painful thoughts and feelings. One way to help them get started with this is by using a simple activity—writing down their hopeless thoughts and feelings on leaves or clouds and then imagining them floating away to Jesus. Before a counseling session or intentional conversation, print the "Thoughts and Feelings on Leaves in a River Floating to Jesus" worksheet or the "Thoughts and Feelings: Crying Out to God" worksheet. Many teens struggle with how difficult it is to stop thinking negative, hopeless thoughts once those feelings begin. You can introduce this exercise as a way to help teens learn how to give their depressed thoughts and feelings to Jesus. Ask them to take time to be silent and allow their negative thoughts and feelings to enter their minds. Then instruct them to write those thoughts and feelings down on the leaves or the clouds printed on the paper and imagine them moving away from them, floating down the river or up into the sky to Jesus—the one who knows them so well. Ask them to imagine watching each of them floating away.

After completing the exercise, remind them that the Bible says that "Even before a word is on my tongue, behold, O Lord, you know it altogether" (Psalm 139:4). We are not doing these activities because God is unaware of our thoughts and feelings, but to help us remember that we can give them to him because he cares for us (1 Peter 5:7). Also, reflect and discuss together how this experience was for them.

Name: ______________________________ Date: ______________

Thoughts and Feelings on Leaves in a River Floating to Jesus

Then the angel showed me the river of the water of life, bright as crystal, flowing from the throne of God and of the Lamb. (Revelation 22:1)

Name: ______________________________ Date: ______________

Thoughts and Feelings: Crying Out to God

Even before a word is on my tongue, behold, O LORD, you know it altogether. (Psalm 139:4)

What does depression say and what does God say? activity[10]

This is an activity that we can do alongside teens struggling with depression. Make sure to have copies of both the "What Does Depression Say About Who God Is and Who I Am?" worksheet and the "What Does God Say About Himself and Who I Am in Christ?" worksheet for this activity. You can read the following or paraphrase it as you begin the activity:

> Your depression says that these feelings of shame, guilt, and thinking that you are never enough, that you've failed, are true. These awful feelings and painful moments lead you to wish you could simply disappear. You gather evidence in this fallen world that yells out you'll never be good enough. Living in this fallen world, these experiences feel like they are true.

Then ask the teen to take their time and write all that their depression says about who God is and who they are on the "What Does Depression Say About Who God Is and Who I Am?" worksheet.

After taking time to talk and reflect together on what their depression is saying about who God is and who they are, you can move on to the second part of the activity. You can read or say something along these lines:

> While you live in this world that is not your home, you will experience real shame, guilt, and darkness that clouds; but what is even more real is that you are covered and clothed with Christ because of his death and resurrection. By his grace, you have been made a new creation. This world is passing away, and although you might feel exposed, shameful, and raw, the reality is that you have been clothed with Christ!

Name: ______________________________ Date: ______________

What Does Depression Say About Who God Is and Who I Am? (Part 1)

> Galatians 3:26–27 says, "So in Christ Jesus you are all children of God through faith, for all of you who were baptized into Christ have clothed yourselves with Christ" (NIV). By faith, we have been clothed with Christ—this is true even when we don't feel this way.
>
> At the same time, Ephesians 4:21–24 says, "assuming that you have heard about him and were taught in him, as the truth is in Jesus, to put off your old self, which belongs to your former manner of life and is corrupt through deceitful desires, and to be renewed in the spirit of your minds, and to put on the new self, created after the likeness of God in true righteousness and holiness." When we receive this gift of being clothed with Christ, God also calls us to be active participants—to put off our old self and to put on our new self.

You can then invite the teenager to practice putting on the clothing of Christ in the midst of their depression by completing the "What Does God Say About Himself and Who I Am in Christ?" worksheet. Together, write down the truth of who God is and how Jesus has clothed us in Christ and reflect on what this means for them in their depression.

Name: ______________________________ Date: ______________

What Does God Say About Himself and Who I Am in Christ? (Part 2)

So in Christ Jesus you are all children of God through faith, for all of you who were baptized into Christ have clothed yourselves with Christ. (Galatians 3:26–27)

Engaging support: don't go it alone activity[11]

While this is an exercise you can do when meeting with a teenager struggling in various ways, it is particularly important for teenagers who suffer with depression to help them identify who they can reach out to for support. Those who are depressed typically want to isolate themselves, will not want to bother or be bothered by anyone, and will consequently make their world smaller and smaller. So, talking to them about others who they can invite into their struggle as they work through their depression will be helpful. When starting this activity, you can begin by reading The Message version of Ecclesiastes 4:9–12, which is on the "Engaging Support: Don't Go It Alone" worksheet. As you discuss who the teenager can include in their support system, an important support to have them consider is someone at the teenager's school, such as a particular teacher, guidance counselor, or school psychologist. Teenagers spend a lot of time at school, and it might be during the school day when they start feeling more down and hopeless—whether because something difficult happened or they were having a bad day. Having a safe person or place to quickly get support can be helpful. While working with many teenagers with depression, I (Monica) have heard many express how helpful it was for them to either take a quick break in their guidance counselor's office or to open up to one of their favorite teachers. As you identify people who can support them, discuss how to have the initial conversation letting them know about their depression and asking for support, as well as what kinds of specific support each person might be able to provide. Also discuss ways the teen can help themselves remember to reach out to these supports when they're struggling, because often when we're depressed the last thing we want to do is remember our supports.

Name: ______________________________ Date: ______________

Engaging Social Support: Don't Go It Alone

It's better to have a partner than go it alone. Share the work, share the wealth. And if one falls down, the other helps, but if there's no one to help, tough! Two in a bed warm each other. Alone, you shiver all night. By yourself you're unprotected. With a friend you can face the worst. Can you round up a third? A three-stranded rope isn't easily snapped. (Ecclesiastes 4:9–12 MSG)

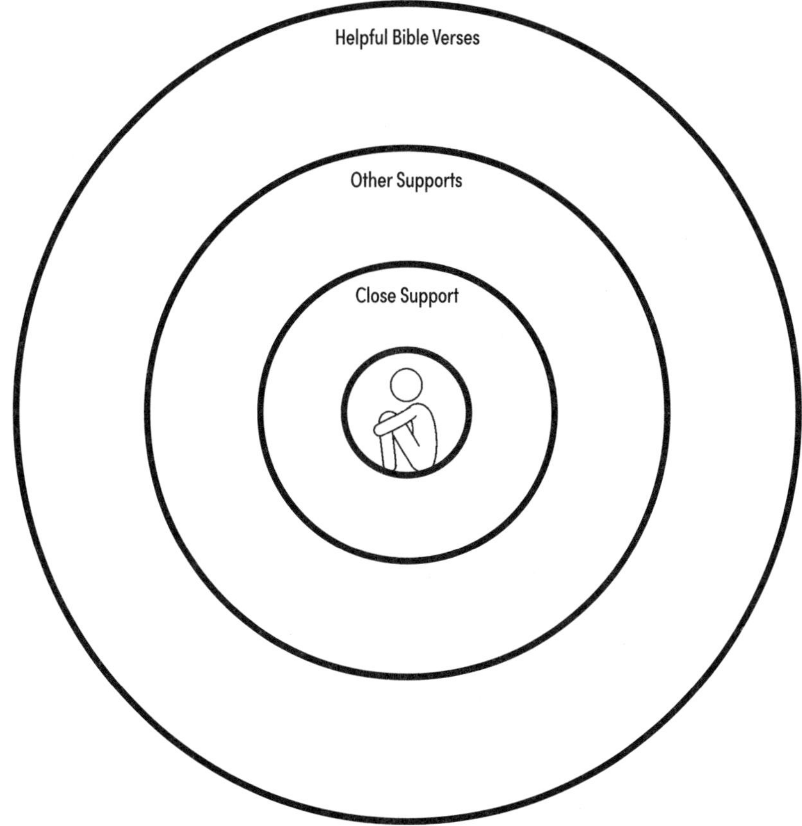

Daily journaling exercises

Consider having a supply of notebooks to encourage a teenager who has depression to journal. We don't want to make it a burden, like another piece of homework to accomplish; instead, our aim is to introduce it to them in a way that encourages them to feel safe. We tell them that the journal is just between them and the Lord, who knows their thoughts even before they have them or write them down. Sometimes teens with depression need some guidance to get them started. A helpful exercise is a daily thankfulness journal, which you could even do with the teen in the beginning. You can get them started by asking them to write, "God, I am thankful for . . . " and listing in detail several things they are thankful for. Taking our eyes off the things that discourage us and placing them on the good gifts God has given is a lifelong practice that can lift our spirits.

Another journaling idea is similar to the "What Does Depression Say and What Does God Say?" activity.[12] Have them draw a line down the middle of a page in their journal, creating two columns. Start by asking them, "What does depression say about who you are?" Have them list those statements in one column. Give them time to think, allowing them to sit in the silence of their thoughts and feelings and write down as much as they can. After they complete this step, ask them, if they are comfortable, to slowly read aloud what they have written. Then ask them how they feel after reading it aloud or silently to themselves. As they reflect and share, express empathy. Don't immediately try to challenge them and tell them that what they wrote about themselves is wrong. Stay in the sadness and heaviness of depression with them. Then, in the second column, start to generate together who they remember God says they are in Christ. You may help them get started by coming up with an alternative truth from the Bible for each of their depressed statements in the first column. As you and the teen continue to come up with alternative truths that challenge the statements of depression, ask them to reflect on their reactions in light of the contrasts and share them. Be slow to speak and quick to listen; share your thoughts and reactions when helpful.

One more type of journaling activity involves taking every thought captive to Christ to remember that the Holy Spirit enables us to do the good work that he has prepared for us beforehand (Ephesians 2:10), even when we feel we cannot. Coach the teen to realize that instead of saying, "Because I am depressed, I *can't* do this, I *can't* do that," they can say, "I can be depressed *and* get out of bed," "I can be depressed *and* go to school," "I can be depressed *and* go out with my youth group," "I can be depressed *and* eat lunch," "I can be depressed *and* take a shower," and so on. Helping the teen remember that being depressed does not prevent them from taking small, doable steps (as much as it might feel that way) is an important part of helping them learn how to live by faith, not by sight.

The Benefits of Good Habits

While as Christians we understand that the greatest hope and healing for depression comes from the gospel, we also know that as embodied souls, teenagers struggling with depression also benefit from receiving other good gifts of God. Studies show that getting regular exercise can help prevent anxiety and depression. People who are more active tend to have fewer symptoms and better overall mental health.[13] Furthermore, maintaining good sleep habits and spending time with friends also helps with depression.[14] Also, healthy eating habits as well as engaging in wise use of social media will be helpful for teen depression. Studies show that good eating habits (e.g., eating fruits and vegetables or having a meal as a family) was found to be linked to better teen psychological well-being, while consumption of sugary drinks was associated with greater severity of depression, particularly in adolescent boys.[15] For specific ways on how parents, pastors, and leaders can help teens develop wiser uses of social media, see chapter 14. As we point teens to the hope we have in Christ through our conversations and help them develop better ways of responding to their depression, let us not forget to also have conversations with them about their daily habits and how those might be supporting or undermining their mental health.

Warning Signs for When Additional Help Is Needed

As parents, pastors, and youth leaders care for teenagers struggling with depression, it will be helpful to consider when you might need to enlarge the circle of care and start talking about the need for additional support with the teenager. Here are warning signs to consider when additional help is needed:[16]

- Often feeling sad, anxious, worthless, or even "empty"
- Loss of interest in activities teenager used to enjoy
- Easily frustrated, irritable, or angry
- Withdrawing from friends and family
- Grades dropping
- Changes in eating or sleeping habits
- Experiencing fatigue or memory loss
- Thoughts about suicide or harming themselves

Although knowing the warning signs are helpful, it might be hard to understand the severity of a teenager's depression. Along with considering these warning signs for when additional help might be needed, parents, pastors, and leaders can use a very simple questionnaire to check for the teenager's level of severity of depression (see p. 134). This is a helpful tool that does not require any training to use. This depression questionnaire is a publicly accessible short questionnaire developed by Drs. Robert L. Spitzer, Janet B. W. Williams, Kurt Kroenke, and colleagues.[17] Through research, it has been found to be a helpful tool to identify the intensity of a teenager's struggle with depression.

The questionnaire is made up of nine questions that asks the teenager to reflect on their experiences of depression over the past two weeks. You can either ask the questions to the teenager or you can make a copy of the questionnaire and have the teenager complete it. Each question asks the teenager to identify a number on a scale of 0 (not at all) to 3 (nearly every day). Once the questionnaire is completed, calculate the total score. If the score is 10 or higher, that could indicate that enlarging the circle of care can be wise and more help is needed. Also, if the teenager answered question 9, "Thoughts that you would be better off dead, or of hurting yourself in some way," with a 1, 2, or 3, it is essential to do a suicide risk assessment (see chapter 13).

If you are a parent, this increased circle of care and support might involve going to your pediatrician to talk about your teen's depression and hearing their thoughts or recommendations. It might involve reaching out to schoolteachers, school counselors, and school psychologists to see how they can provide support for your depressed teen while they are at school. It might mean helping them receive formal counseling from a mental health professional.

Finding Rest Amid the Heaviness

Depression in teenagers can become laborious, heavily burdensome, and unrelenting. As parents, pastors, and youth leaders who love teenagers draw near to them, you can offer the hope of the gospel in the present moment through your compassionate relationship and various practical activities. As you minister to their weary hearts, remember also that you are not alone. Remember that you too can go to Jesus amid the heaviness and find rest in Jesus who said,

> "Come to me, all who labor and are heavy laden, and I will give you rest. Take my yoke upon you, and learn from me, for I am gentle and lowly in heart, and you will find rest for

your souls. For my yoke is easy, and my burden is light." (Matthew 11:28–30)

Figure 4: Depression Questionnaire

During the past two weeks, how often have you been bothered by the following problems?

	Not at all	Several days	More than half the days	Nearly every day
1. Feeling down, depressed, irritable, or hopeless?	0	1	2	3
2. Little interest or pleasure in doing things?	0	1	2	3
3. Trouble fallling asleep, staying asleep, or sleeping too much?	0	1	2	3
4. Poor appetite, weight loss, or overeating?	0	1	2	3
5. Feeling tired or having little energy?	0	1	2	3
6. Feeling bad about yourself—or feeling that you are a failure, or that you have let yourself or your family down?	0	1	2	3
7. Trouble concentrating on things like schoolwork, reading, or watching online?	0	1	2	3
8. Moving or speaking so slowly that other people could have noticed? Or the opposite—being so fidgety or restless that you were moving around a lot more than usual?	0	1	2	3
9. Thoughts that you would be better off dead, or of hurting yourself in some way?	0	1	2	3
Total Score: ______ = Add columns:		______ +	______ +	______

(Source: Developed by Drs. Robert L. Spitzer, Janet B. W. Williams, Kurt Kroenke, and colleagues; no permission required)

CHAPTER 9

Teenagers with Body Image Issues and Eating Disorders

Clara's parents noticed that she had begun to regularly skip meals and she would often say she was overweight, even though she was not. Clara talked excessively about food, dieting, and the number of calories in a particular food, and she made sure to read the nutrition facts before purchasing or consuming a particular food. When these changes first began, Clara's mom was not alarmed since Clara's body was beginning to develop more as a teenager, and she thought it was just a typical reaction to these changes. She thought Clara would soon accept that her body's changes were normal. However, what first appeared to be picky eating developed into avoiding meals or just pushing food around on her plate, taking a few bites, but not eating nearly enough food. Clara's weight loss was beginning to alarm her parents. Clara also became more withdrawn and quieter, even though she was typically a shy teenager. Her mood seemed to be more consistently down. Eventually Clara's mom found out that she was restricting her food so much that she had stopped menstruating during her monthly cycle.

In our fallen world, there is so much focus on how we look. In American culture in particular, this focus on external appearances has led to widespread dieting, because being thin or having a particular kind of body shape is viewed as a primary marker of health and appeal. Because dieting and caring about one's weight is so pervasive, it can be difficult to recognize when a teenager's thinking or behavior has become destructive and even dangerous. Body image issues or body dissatisfaction tend to start in adolescence. Studies find that a significant proportion of teenagers experience body image issues. Approximately 24 to 46 percent of adolescent girls and 12 to 26 percent of adolescent boys have reported dissatisfaction with their bodies.[1] Many engage in weight management practices, with up to 60 percent dieting regularly, and over 50 percent exercising specifically to change their body shape. For about 70 percent of teenage girls, body shape is a key factor in determining self-esteem.[2] For teenage boys, muscularity was a key factor linked to their self-esteem.[3] Although body image issues are very common among teens, more severe eating disorders are less common, and their prevalence differs by type, gender, and age. Body image issues may lead to disordered eating.[4]

Although there are a wide variety of possible eating disorders, this chapter will focus on anorexia nervosa (AN) and bulimia nervosa (BN). AN is a condition that involves persistent restriction of food relative to body weight, which over time leads to significantly low body weight.[5] When someone is suffering from AN, they intensely fear gaining weight or becoming fat, so they will take drastic action to prevent weight gain. In addition, those struggling with AN have a difficult time accurately perceiving their own body size and typically see themselves as normal or overweight when they are actually emaciated.

BN is a condition in which individuals eat a large amount of food at one time while feeling a lack of control, which is then followed by compensatory behaviors (i.e., self-induced vomiting; excessive exercise; misuse of laxatives, diuretics, or other medications; and fasting). To be diagnosed with BN, these episodes of binge eating followed by compensatory behaviors happen at least once per week for several months. Someone struggling with BN has their sense of self unduly influenced by body shape and weight.

AN affects around 0.3 percent of adolescents, while BN impacts between 0.9 percent.[6] Though these numbers may seem low, these conditions tend to be chronic. Approximately 58 percent of teenagers with AN and 72 percent of teenagers with BN struggle with it throughout their lifetime. Broken down according to gender, 0.3 percent of both teen girls and teen boys are impacted by AN. Concerning BN, 1.3 percent of teen girls and 0.5 percent of teen boys are affected by it.[7] Eating disorders often arise during adolescence and early adulthood; for example, the typical age of onset for AN is between fourteen and eighteen years. BN usually shows up later, in late adolescence and early adulthood.[8]

There are various ways in which a person develops an eating disorder. Hundreds of studies that were aggregated together have found the following risk factors.[9] It can be shaped by a perfectionistic personality (AN), impulsiveness (BN), a history of mood or anxiety conditions, and stressful life events. Other familial, social, and cultural factors can exacerbate eating disorders, such as parental teasing about weight, pressure to conform to ideal body types, and exposure to thin ideals in media. While the exact extent of this media influence remains unclear, the cultural pressure to conform to these beauty standards is pervasive. In addition, involvement in elite sports and certain activities like ballet, modeling, and wrestling, which emphasize maintaining a specific body shape or weight, are linked to higher risks of eating disorders. A meta-analysis that was included in the aggregated study showed that genetic susceptibility can also contribute to the likelihood of developing an eating disorder. Finally, adolescence is a critical risk period, as body changes can heighten feelings of insecurity and self-loathing; early puberty was found to be linked to the development of eating disorders.

Eating disorders can result in severe medical complications, particularly due to malnutrition. Individuals with AN may suffer from hypothermia, anemia, impaired kidney function, low blood pressure, low heart rate, and damage to the structure and function of the heart.[10] Chronic malnourishment can even lead to brain damage, osteoporosis, and delayed puberty.[11] For those with BN, the issues are often related to purging behaviors, such as vomiting and laxative misuse. These behaviors can result in electrolyte imbalances, worn tooth enamel, tooth decay, esophageal damage, acid reflux disorder, severe dehydration, and even heart complications like arrhythmias.[12] Thus, because there is real risk of significant physical harm, it is imperative that those who struggle with these disorders receive expert help as soon as possible.

I (Monica) have been on many diets and I've grappled with my own body image, particularly during my teenage years. However, an eating disorder is more than a typical struggle with body image. I have seen teenagers and their families come in for help for chronic and more serious eating disorders which, if untreated, can wreck lives, harm relationships, and interfere with accomplishing future goals. The suffering involved in an eating disorder can last a long time, and some sufferers might require hospitalization. As we have ministered to teenagers at church, many have shared their fears and alarm for their close friends at school who were secretly suffering from an eating disorder. As a pastor or lay leader, you might not directly journey with teenagers who struggle acutely, but an important way to care is being aware of how the condition can affect teenagers' and their families' lives. This awareness can raise more compassion, enabling the church and youth ministry to be an inviting place for sufferers to share their secrets and ask for help. As a church or youth ministry, we can raise awareness and educate by displaying resources such as Laurie Daily-Murphy's handout, "What to Say, What Not to Say"[13] (see p. 152) or a minibook like Ed Welch's *Eating Disorders: The Quest for Thinness*.[14]

The Gospel Amid Body Image Issues and Eating Disorders: Glorifying God in Our Body

If we do know a teen struggling with AN or BN, even after we help them get the appropriate medical help they need, we can minister to the spiritual aspects of their struggle and also grow in addressing the far more common struggle with body image among all of the teens under our care. Paul in 1 Corinthians 6:12–13 says, "'All things are lawful for me,' but not all things are helpful. 'All things are lawful for me,' but I will not be dominated by anything. 'Food is meant for the stomach and the stomach for food'—and God will destroy both one and the other." While this passage was written in the context of admonishing the Corinthian church to flee from sexual immorality and to remember that the body is a temple of the Holy Spirit, this passage can also remind us how we can become dominated by anything, even by food. Paul says further, "You are not your own, for you were bought with a price. So glorify God in your body" (1 Corinthians 6:19–20). This is a critical reminder that the believing teenager's body was bought at a costly price; their body does not belong to themselves, but to God. This is good news for teenagers struggling with dissatisfaction with their bodies or eating disorders. While their flesh wages war through shame, fear, or desires for control, because struggling teenagers are united to Christ, God is not ashamed of their bodies, even if they are! Furthermore, in 2 Corinthians 5:1, Paul likens our earthly bodies to a tent, saying, "For we know that if the tent that is our earthly home is destroyed, we have a building from God, a house not made with hands, eternal in the heavens." Teenagers struggling with body image issues or eating disorders can be reminded of this great hope they have in Christ.

Providing Compassionate Care: Drawing Near and Being With

For teenagers, dissatisfaction about their bodies can be hard to face alone. For some teenagers, body image issues can lead to eating disorders, so it is important to deal with their dissatisfaction with their bodies. In this section we'll share practical activities that a parent, pastor, or youth leader can use to help teenagers deal with their body image issues and understand how the gospel gives a better way. It is important to note that we only recommend using these activities *after* you have built a strong relationship with the teen and listened carefully to deeply understand the nature of their specific struggle (for advice on how to do this effectively, see chapter 4, especially the sections on building relationships and listening carefully). Once you have done this foundational work, you can use your wisdom to select an exercise that can be helpful to them in specific ways.

Writing negative thoughts and feelings about my body on leaves floating to Jesus[15]

An important tool for teenagers to help manage or deal with their body image issues is to practice crying out to God with their negative thoughts and feelings about their body. One way to help them get started with this is by using a simple activity—writing down their harsh negative thoughts and feelings on leaves or clouds and then imagining them floating away to Jesus. Teenagers' dissatisfaction with their bodies can often involve negative perceptions of their shape and physical appearance. It can include negative perceptions of their skin color, physical features, ability, muscularity, and gender identity. Body image issues often come with feelings of shame, anxiety, and self-consciousness. Teenagers who experience high levels of body dissatisfaction often feel their bodies are flawed in comparison to others.[16] Before a counseling session or intentional conversation, print the "Negative Thoughts and Feelings About My Body on Leaves in a River Floating to Jesus" worksheet or the "Negative Thoughts and Feelings About My Body: Crying Out to God" worksheet.

Many teens find it difficult to stop thinking negative thoughts once those bad feelings begin. You can introduce this exercise as a way to help teens learn how to give their harsh, negative thoughts and feelings to Jesus. Ask them to take time to be silent and allow these negative thoughts and feelings to enter their minds. Then instruct them to write them down on the leaves or clouds printed on the paper and imagine them moving away from them, floating down the river or up into the sky to Jesus—the one who created them. Ask them to imagine watching each of them floating away.

After completing the exercise, remind them that the Bible says that "Even before a word is on my tongue, behold, O Lord, you know it altogether" (Psalm 139:4). We are not doing these activities because God is unaware of our thoughts and feelings, but to help us remember that we can give them to him because he cares for us (1 Peter 5:7). Reflect and discuss together how this experience was for them.

Name: ________________________________ Date: ______________

Thoughts and Feelings on Leaves in a River Floating to Jesus

Then the angel showed me the river of the water of life, bright as crystal, flowing from the throne of God and of the Lamb. (Revelation 22:1)

Name: ______________________________ Date: ______________

Thoughts and Feelings: Crying Out to God

Even before a word is on my tongue, behold, O LORD,
you know it altogether. (Psalm 139:4)

Made in God's image exercise[17]

Here's another exercise you can do with teenagers who struggle with body image issues. Before a counseling session or intentional conversation, print the "Made in God's Image: Fearfully and Wonderfully Made" worksheet. Teenagers who struggle with their body image may stay overly focused on their bodies. This exercise will encourage them to look up to the creative handiwork of God who has wonderfully made them in his image. Even though the teenager may feel intense dissatisfaction with their bodies, help them remember what Scripture says about how God made them by reflecting on the following passages together:

> So God created man in his own image, in the image of God he created him; male and female he created them. (Genesis 1:27)

> I praise you, for I am fearfully and wonderfully made. Wonderful are your works; my soul knows it very well. (Psalm 139:14)

After reflecting together on these passages, use the worksheet to help the teenager give careful thought to and write down (inside the outline of the body) the positive aspects of their body that reflects God's handiwork. After the teenager has written as many aspects as they can, move on to the next part of this activity, which focuses on how God has skillfully created believing teenagers for good works through redemption in Christ. Read and reflect on this passage together:

> For by grace you have been saved through faith. And this is not your own doing; it is the gift of God, not a result of works, so that no one may boast. For we are his

> workmanship, created in Christ Jesus for good works, which God prepared beforehand, that we should walk in them. (Ephesians 2:8–10)

Then reflect and discuss together how Christ has skillfully made the teenager to do good works. Help the teenager to reflect on some of their strengths and talents that can be used for good and instruct them to write those strengths and talents in the blank spaces around the image of the body. After completing the exercise, reflect and discuss together how this experience was for them.

Name: ______________________________ Date: ______________

Made in God's Image: Fearfully and Wonderfully Made

So God created man in his own image, in the image of God he created him; male and female he created them. (Genesis 1:27)

I praise you, for I am fearfully and wonderfully made. Wonderful are your works; my soul knows it very well. (Psalm 319:14)

Writing a letter to the body negativity voices (BNV)

This exercise invites the struggling teenager to externalize the body negativity voices by writing a letter to them. While giving instructions to write this letter, read together the following passage:

> Fear not, for you will not be ashamed; be not confounded, for you will not be disgraced . . . no weapon that is fashioned against you shall succeed, and you shall refute every tongue that rises against you in judgment. (Isaiah 54:4, 17)

Then invite the struggling teenager to write a letter to their BNV and to include in the letter all the things you despise about the BNV. Tell the BNV how they have harmed you and affected your life. Tell the BNV how life would be better without all the attacks. Then help the teenager to tell the BNV in this letter about the truths of God that refute the judgmental lies the voices are raising against the Christian teenager. This activity can be done repeatedly as the teenager struggles with body image issues.

Reducing social media use

While parents, pastors, and lay leaders cannot control how media (television, movies, advertisements, etc.) or social media (Facebook, Instagram, TikTok, YouTube, Snapchat, etc.) portrays the ideal body (e.g., thin or muscular), what we know is that these ideals do perpetuate weight stigma, which has been shown to increase the likelihood of experiencing body dissatisfaction as mentioned in this chapter. One research study found that both male and female youths who reduced social media use to one hour per day found a significant reduction in negative body image issues.[18] This finding suggests that helping teenagers devise a plan to reduce social media use may be a wise and loving approach to caring for those struggling with body image issues.

Considering parental example

Parents can love their teenager who may be struggling with their body image by setting an example of how to treat one's own body well—as a temple of the living Lord. Parents, your negative comments about your own bodies and your excessive exercise or restrictive dieting can unintentionally influence your teenager's body image. Also, as mentioned before, parents' teasing or critical commentary about a teenager's appearance or pressures to lose weight can affect the teen's negativity about their body.

Warning Signs for When Additional Help Is Needed[19]

There are many signs that show a teenager may be at risk of developing an eating disorder. By being aware of these early warning signs, teenagers and their families or caregivers can begin to take action to prevent an eating disorder from worsening. Remember that not all warning signs means a teenager has a severe eating disorder, and that it is not our job to diagnose anyone, but if there are several of these signs present, they warrant taking the teen to someone who can make a diagnosis. Here are some behavior and emotional warning signs to consider:

- **Dissatisfaction with body shape or weight**: Constant complaints about their body or wanting to change their appearance
- **Skipping meals or fasting**: Regularly avoiding meals or fasting for extended periods (such as twenty-four hours or more)
- **Private eating**: Preferring to eat alone rather than in public or with family
- **Strange eating habits**: Cutting food into tiny pieces, chewing for unusually long periods, or organizing food in specific ways

- **Binging and purging**: Sudden episodes of overeating followed by fasting or feeling guilty about food intake
- **Food avoidance and selective choices**: Regularly choosing low-fat, low-carbohydrate foods, or adopting a restrictive diet like vegetarianism without medical reasons
- **Extreme concern with calories**: Constantly reading food labels, following strict diet plans, or rigidly applying weight-loss programs
- **Anxiety after eating**: Feeling physically or emotionally uncomfortable after meals due to calorie concerns

Additional signs of Anorexia Nervosa (AN) can include:

- **Excessive weight loss**: Losing weight to dangerous levels or below a healthy range for their age and size
- **Odd food rituals**: Engaging in unusual behaviors around food, such as eating foods in a specific order or ritualistically preparing meals
- **Menstrual cycle irregularities**: Missing periods (amenorrhea) or other hormonal issues in females
- **Physical changes**: Developing fine hair on the body, especially the face, arms, and torso, which is the body's way of keeping warm due to weight loss
- **Wearing baggy clothes**: Hiding weight loss or body shape.
- **Fainting or dizziness**: Frequent weakness, dizziness, or fainting spells due to lack of nutrition
- **Vigorous exercise at odd hours**: Exercising excessively or at unusual times, such as late at night or early in the morning
- **High need for control**: Striving for perfection, especially related to body image or weight

Additional Signs of Bulimia Nervosa (BN) can include:

- **Missing food**: Large quantities of food disappearing from the home, often consumed during binge-eating episodes
- **Secretive behavior**: Eating in secret or hiding food
- **Weight fluctuations**: Rapid changes in weight due to binging and purging cycles
- **Physical signs from purging**: Frequent trips to the bathroom after meals, cuts or scrapes on the back of the hand from induced vomiting, tooth decay, constant sore throat, swollen glands in the neck, puffy cheeks, or broken blood vessels in eyes
- **Use of diet aids**: Relying on diet pills, laxatives, or other substances to control weight
- **Disparaging talk about food intake**: Speaking negatively about themselves in relation to food or their body size

If you identify warning signs in a teen that warrant additional treatment, you can expect a qualified mental health professional to pursue a multipronged approach. The main goals of treatment will usually include:[20]

1. **Medical care and restoring weight**: Treating the health consequences of an eating disorder, prescribing medication, and helping the individual regain a healthy weight
2. **Changing distorted emotions, thoughts, and eating behaviors**: Addressing unhealthy eating patterns and behaviors around food
3. **Addressing psychological and family issues**: Tackling underlying emotional issues and family dynamics that contribute to the condition

Due to some of the more severe impact of eating disorders on a teenager's body, finding professional help can be crucial. Parents, while getting this type of multipronged approach to your teen's eating disorder, you can enlarge this circle of support by offering to help your teenager understand a Christian perspective on their struggle. Before you offer to enlarge their circle, do some exploration in your area to find a counselor who understands and has experience with eating disorders, knowing the psychological issues and viewing it from a Christian perspective.

Transformed into His Masterpieces

Teenagers struggling with body image and eating disorders need our help as parents, pastors, and youth leaders to see their true identity in God. They are hurting both physically and spiritually, needing to be fed with the true gospel and know they are loved fully, both internally and externally. Ephesians 2:10 reminds us that we are God's workmanship, or in other words, his masterpieces in Christ. May we remember that in Christ, we and teenagers are transformed into his masterpieces, and may we provide that truth and hope to our teenagers.

What to Say, What Not to Say

To Someone in Recovery from an Eating Disorder

By Laurie Daily-Murphy, CEDS, CHT

Below are very good general suggestions for everyone to follow. Our culture is too focused on appearances and this will help you do your part to decrease the number of eating disorders in our society. It will also help your loved one feel more comfortable and supported. Focus on the person and who they are on the inside . . . not on their appearance.

Do Not Say

1. Do not make weight gain or weight loss comments.
2. Do not make comments about appearance on body size.
3. Do not talk about how much food they eat or don't eat.
4. Do not touch her body parts in a way to draw attention to them.
5. Do not talk about your own dieting or weight obsession.
6. Do not talk about others body size or weight.
7. Do not say "you look healthy," to them it means "you look fat."
8. Do not talk about how fast or slow they eat.
9. Do not talk about heavy or upsetting topics during meals.
10. Do not talk about what food choices they are making.
11. Do not label foods "good" or "bad." All foods are OK and fuel for the body.
12. Do not say that this illness is just an attempt to get attention . . . it's not.

Do Say

1. Do ask them how they are doing and feeling . . . then LISTEN without disregarding their emotions.
2. Do tell them you are proud of them for facing this issue.
3. Do tell them you are here to support them and ask them how you might be of support.
4. Do use empathy and kindness.
5. Do ask them about how their day was.
6. Do ask them what they are experiencing on a day-to-day basis.
7. Do talk to them about their interests and activities.
8. Do keep the conversations at meals positive and lighthearted. Talk about things other than food or eating.
9. Do compliment them based on their personality or character.
10. If you feel concerned that someone is slipping back into old patterns, talk to them honestly with empathy and love—not judgment.
11. Do make similar comments and compliments like:

    I love you.
    I love having you here.
    I enjoy your company.
    You are a beautiful person.
    You are glowing.
    You are growing and learning and it's wonderful to see.
    I love how brave you were to deal with this head-on.

(Source: Used with permission from Laurie Daily-Murphy)

CHAPTER 10

Teenagers with Substance Use Issues

On many occasions over the years, teenagers in our youth group would come to us needing community service hours. Sometimes they needed to get hours for school service requirements or to try to get into the National Honor Society at their schools. However, on some occasions, a teenager would come to us because they had gotten in trouble. In particular, we can recall cases where a teenager was caught driving under the influence and they needed community service hours mandated by the courts to get their sentence expunged or erased. Moreover, we can recall one circumstance where the same teenager came to us a second time because they were convicted again for drunk driving. This time, the community service hours were not to expunge their record but as part of their plea deal so they would not have to go to jail. After hearing from him and his parents about what was going on, we knew this teenager was not just drinking and driving as a random one-time mistake, but he had a recurring problem with alcohol abuse.

National US statistics of high school students reveal that 23 percent currently drink alcohol, 14 percent have binge drunk in the last 30 days, 17 percent have ridden in a vehicle driven by someone who has been drinking alcohol in the last 30 days, 16 percent currently use marijuana, and 18 percent currently use an electronic vapor product.[1] During adolescence, there is an increased desire for new and intense experiences, which can lead to risk-taking behaviors. For example, although teenagers tend to drink alcohol less often than adults, they tend to drink more when they do drink (e.g., binge drinking, defined as five or more drinks on one occasion).[2] In addition, research shows that teenagers are more likely to engage in risky behaviors when they are with peers, such that peer presence can diminish cognitive control and increase the temptation to use substances.[3] As they grow older, teenagers generally become more capable of resisting peer pressure.

Not every teenager who experiments with addictive substances develops a dependency, but some do. While many teenagers will experiment a great deal with drugs and alcohol, only a minority will become dependent upon them, which is reassuring to know.[4] According to the Substance Abuse and Mental Health Services Administration (SAMHSA), 27.2 million people, or 9.6 percent of Americans aged twelve and older, needed help in 2023 for substance use disorders.[5] Illicit drug use tends to peak in late adolescence; approximately 18 percent of young adults aged eighteen to twenty-five have a substance use disorder. The report also showed that 6.9 percent of teenagers aged twelve to seventeen years old have a substance use disorder.[6]

Many teenagers who develop a dependency can face long-term challenges. For example, long-term marijuana use has been linked to negative educational and life outcomes, such as ongoing relationship problems.[7] Substance abuse can also lead to severe health issues. For example, methamphetamine is known to cause significant brain damage and cognitive deficits, although some recovery may occur after prolonged abstinence.[8] More and more research is showing that drinking alcohol earlier, as a teenager, may have significant impact on cognitive function, memory, and school performance over time—maybe even into adulthood.[9] Research has found that starting substance use at a young age heightens the risk of addiction later.[10]

Having a substance use issue involves compulsively using a substance despite experiencing negative consequences. Often the teen will realize that they have been gradually taking the substance in larger amounts or more consistently over a longer period of time than they should, so they will desire and try to cut back their use, but they will be unsuccessful in their efforts. Due to continued use of a substance, they likely have developed tolerance and will need greater amounts of the substance to achieve the desired effect or to prevent withdrawal symptoms. In addition, as their dependency increases, they will spend a great deal of time obtaining, using, or recovering from the substance's effects, and so they will experience various subsequent impairments, including health problems and failure to meet major responsibilities at work, school, or home.

Many factors increase the likelihood of substance use issues among teenagers. Teenagers are exposed to a lot of content about substance use on social media, with an increase in the number of posts about vaping.[11] It has been found that social media content around alcohol and tobacco can influence substance use among teenagers.[12] Furthermore, associating with peers who abuse substances is a strong predictor of adolescent substance use. Other factors, like lack of parental supervision, family conflict, and a family history of substance abuse, contribute to risk of use. Additionally, teenagers who struggle with various other mental health conditions may be more susceptible to use. Amid all these factors that may lead to the misuse of substances, Christian teenagers are not only sufferers, but also sinners. James 1:14 says that "But each person is tempted when he is lured and enticed by his own desire." While it is illegal in the US for anyone under the age of twenty-one to use alcohol, tobacco, or marijuana, or medication without a prescription, many teenagers still use. Teenagers may be tempted, enticed by their own desires, to misuse substances to fit in with their peers, to boost confidence, or as an escape or instant relief from bad feelings (e.g., anxious, depressed, boredom, or loneliness).

While there are many factors that can lead to substance use and addiction, conversely, certain factors can help prevent substance abuse. These include close, supportive relationships with parents;[13] active involvement in school academics and extracurricular activities;[14] engagement in positive community activities and religious organizations;[15] and delaying the onset of substance use. Research indicates that each year of delayed use significantly reduces the likelihood of future dependence.[16]

Engaging with teenagers in a supportive manner and fostering open communication can greatly influence their choices regarding drugs and alcohol. Don't be afraid to talk about the issues honestly, sharing your concerns with grace and truth. Parents' responses to their children's substance use vary widely, from strict opposition to more permissive attitudes. It's essential for parents to engage in open discussions about drugs and alcohol, establish clear expectations, and maintain watchfulness and attentiveness. Parents, if you are noticing that your teenager is most likely using, when you confront the teenager, you can do it in a strong but supportive manner, expressing your love and care for them. Caregivers should be aware of their own behaviors, as teenagers often model their actions.

The Gospel Amid Substance Use Issues: Walk by the Spirit

Scripture speaks into the excessive use of alcohol. Galatians 5:1 says, "For freedom Christ has set us free; stand firm therefore, and do not submit again to a yoke of slavery." Christian teenagers have been set free through Christ. But Paul warns Christians to not use this freedom "as an opportunity for the flesh, but through love serve one another" (5:13), encouraging us to "walk by the Spirit, and you will not gratify the desires of the flesh" (5:16). Paul then lists the works of the flesh, which include drunkenness. The call for Christian teenagers who struggle with substance use issues and are gratifying the desires of their flesh are admonished, then encouraged to instead walk by the Spirit. And "the fruit of the Spirit is love, joy, peace, patience, kindness, goodness, faithfulness, gentleness, self-control" (5:22–23). The good news is teenagers who belong to Christ Jesus have crucified the flesh with its passions and desires (5:24). As we walk with teenagers who are struggling with substance abuse, we can remind them that Christ has died to set them free from sin and all its entrapments.

Providing Compassionate Care: Drawing Near and Being With

It is important to note that we only recommend using these activities *after* you have built a strong relationship with the teen and listened carefully to deeply understand the nature of their specific struggle with substance use (for advice on how to do this effectively, see chapter 4, especially the sections on building relationships and listening carefully). Once you have done this foundational work, you can use your wisdom to select an exercise that can be helpful to them in specific ways. Some teenagers might not be willing to get outside help. If teenagers are coming to you, the tools here can be something that parents, pastors, or leaders use to encourage teenagers to make changes to their substance use behaviors. Many teenagers who struggle with substance use issues will be ambivalent about reducing/stopping. A way to help teenagers with this ambivalence is to encourage them to talk about it—engage in change talk. The activities below may help you to support teenagers talk about changing their substance use behaviors.

Importance scale

This importance scale can be used before and after any of the following activities. Tell the teenager that you would like to know how important they think it is to stop or reduce their substance use. You can then ask them the following questions:

- On a scale of 0 to 10, where 0 = not at all and 10 = totally convinced, how convinced are you that it is important for you to stop or reduce using?
- What makes you say [number]?
- Why did you say [number] and not [lower number]?
- What would make it move to a [higher number]?

Talk about safety issues: Care for others and themselves

After you have listened well and understood the teenager's substance use issues (e.g., what substances they use, when they started using, why they are using, or how much they use) in an intentional conversation, invite them to talk about safety concerns. Ask them if they have thought about safety issues when using (e.g., driving while under the influence of substances or excessive harmful substance use) and if they have, what steps they are taking to ensure safety for themselves and others. Explore together further steps needed to address any safety issues (how they can make it safe for themselves and others) by coming up with concrete plans (e.g., I will only use marijuana in my bedroom when I don't have further plans to drive somewhere).

Writing conflicting thoughts and feelings about my substance use issue on clouds[17]

Many teenagers who struggle with substance use issues will have conflicting thoughts and feelings about reducing or stopping their behavior. One way to help teenagers with this ambivalence is to encourage them to talk about it—engage in change talk. This activity helps teenagers to cry out to God about their conflicting thoughts and feelings. Before a counseling session or intentional conversation, print the "Thoughts and Feelings: Crying Out to God" worksheet (p. 162). Using this worksheet, help teenagers first reflect on their thoughts and feelings about their substance use issues, then encourage them to write them down on the clouds as they float up to God. Prior to the activity, help them remember that "Even before a word is on my tongue, behold, O Lord, you know it altogether" (Psalm 139:4). You might even go further into Psalm 139 by reading and reflecting on verses 7–12 together:

> Where shall I go from your Spirit?
> Or where shall I flee from your presence?

> If I ascend to heaven, you are there!
>   If I make my bed in Sheol, you are there!
> If I take the wings of the morning
>   and dwell in the uttermost parts of the sea,
> even there your hand shall lead me,
>   and your right hand shall hold me.
> If I say, "Surely the darkness shall cover me,
>   and the light about me be night,"
> even the darkness is not dark to you;
>   the night is bright as the day,
>   for darkness is as light with you.

Let them know that we are not doing these activities because God is unaware of our thoughts and feelings. In fact, as Psalm 139 says, even when we want to run and hide, God is with us. This activity is to help us remember that we can give them to him because he cares for us (1 Peter 5:7). After completing the exercise, reflect and discuss together how this experience was for them. If they would like to make changes, discuss these changes by writing down goals and the specific steps they plan to take to reach those goals. In Matthew 7:7–9, Jesus said,

> Ask, and it will be given to you; seek, and you will find; knock, and it will be opened to you. For everyone who asks receives, and the one who seeks finds, and to the one who knocks it will be opened.

Remember to pray with the teenager, asking our gracious Lord for help.

Cost-benefit activity: Choosing to change

On a blank sheet of paper, draw a line down the center and write down the following headings. Then explore, discuss, and jot down what the teenager shared:

- Benefits of maintaining substance use
- Cost of maintaining substance use

After completing that list, on another blank sheet of paper draw a line down the center and write down these headings. Then explore, discuss, and jot down what the teenager shared:

- Benefits of reducing/stopping substance use
- Cost of reducing/stopping substance use

After completing the exercise, reflect and discuss together how this exercise was for them. Ask them how this might help them to start making any changes to their substance use issues. If they would like to make changes, discuss these changes by writing down their goals and the specific steps they plan to take to reach those goals. First John 5:14–15 says, "And this is the confidence that we have toward him, that if we ask anything according to his will he hears us. And if we know that he hears us in whatever we ask, we know that we have the requests that we have asked of him." Remember to pray together with them, asking our gracious Lord for help.

Warning Signs for When Additional Help Is Needed

Recognizing that a teenager has developed a substance use dependency can be challenging due to the typical experimentation that occurs during this developmental stage. In addition, many teenagers deny their usage and do not seek out help. However, by understanding the signs of substance use issues and the various factors that contribute to them, parents, pastors, and leaders can work together to address these issues and support godly, wise choices. Although it may vary depending on the kind of substance the teenager is using, here are a few warning signs:

- **Academic decline**: Poor grades, frequent absences, or tardiness
- **Social changes**: New peer groups, especially older friends, and withdrawal from family
- **Behavioral issues**: Rule-breaking, lying, stealing, mood swings, irritability, and unexpected anger
- **Physical changes**: Noticeable alterations in appearance, such as weight loss or gain, or lack of hygiene
- **Substance-related indicators**: Possession of drug paraphernalia or smoking or vaping

If you discovered that the teen has not only experimented with illegal substance use but is in fact showing signs of dependency, then it is imperative to get them specialized help. For most teenagers, this specialized help will be in the form of an outpatient treatment center or individual therapy with professionals who have expertise in treating substance use issues. Inpatient hospitalization and detoxification is not required for most teenagers but is used for those with severe drug or alcohol dependence. Parents, pastors, and leaders seeking to find treatment centers and individual therapy for teenagers with substance use issues should explore options with the support of trusted friends, church, and others in their area.

All to the Glory of God

As parents, pastors, and youth leaders, working with teenagers struggling with substance use issues can be hard. However, we are called to bring the hope of the gospel to struggling teenagers. As the apostle Paul states in 1 Corinthians 10:31, "So, whether you eat or drink, or whatever you do, do all to the glory of God." May we help teenagers who struggle with substance use see that their lives and bodies, and what they do with their bodies, is for the glory of God.

Name: ______________________________ Date: ______________

Thoughts and Feelings: Crying Out to God

Even before a word is on my tongue, behold, O LORD,
you know it altogether. (Psalm 139:4)

CHAPTER 11
TEENAGERS WITH TRAUMA

About five months ago, Evelyn was in a car accident with her family. Although the car was totaled, Evelyn's family was very thankful to the Lord that none of them were seriously physically hurt. But since then, each time they got in the car, Evelyn would ask which direction they were going, requesting that they avoid the site of the accident. Evelyn's parents noticed that even though they assured her they would not be passing by the site of the accident, she would keep looking out the car window, seeming to be on the lookout for anything that might happen. She was having a hard time relaxing in the car like she used to.

Evelyn also complained to her parents about having trouble sleeping and experiencing nightmares—sometimes of the accident, but sometimes of other scary things that she couldn't remember afterward. She was also having some trouble staying focused at school and became jumpy when her friends would appear around the corner and say, "Hi." Evelyn wondered if something was wrong with her; she felt out of control sometimes.

After experiencing trauma, teenagers may show various emotional, cognitive, and behavioral reactions. These reactions can include irritability, angry outbursts, guilt, shame, difficulty concentrating, negative thinking, trouble sleeping, nightmares, hypervigilance, physical discomfort such as stomachaches, separation anxiety, avoidance of reminders of the trauma (i.e., avoiding thoughts, people, places, or situations), withdrawal from social situations, and engaging in risky behaviors (e.g., substance abuse).[1] These reactions may lessen over time, especially with support and help in learning how to navigate through them. A teenager's response to trauma is closely linked to their developmental stage. While some may show resilience, others may struggle without adequate support. Good social support, both before and after a traumatic event, is significant in helping teenagers recover from trauma. When teenagers talk about their traumatic story or event with a person close to them, they can begin to walk the road to healing and recovery. This is important for parents, pastors, and youth leaders to know so that they can express greater compassion, care, and understanding to teenagers and their families after trauma.

However, for some, symptoms may persist beyond a month, indicating the potential development of post-traumatic stress disorder (PTSD). PTSD symptoms usually develop within three months of a traumatic event but can sometimes take longer to surface. The lifetime prevalence of PTSD in US teenagers is 5 to 8 percent, with girls being generally more likely to experience PTSD than boys. In adults, the prevalence of PTSD in women is nearly double that of men, with rates between 8 and 11 percent for women and around 4 to 5 percent for men. Teenagers who are prone to anxiety and depression seem to be more likely to develop PTSD. In addition, the amount and type of trauma, as well as the duration of exposure, impact how trauma affects the body, mind, and brain.[2]

PTSD affects a teenager's body and mind. The body's stress system (i.e., the hypothalamic-pituitary-adrenal axis and the sympathetic nervous system, commonly known as the fight-flight response) becomes altered after trauma. Trauma can impair the brain's ability to end stress responses and distinguish between safe and unsafe situations. When reminded of the trauma, the emotional-sensory part of the brain is hyperactive, resulting in hypervigilance and an inability to assess threats properly. In addition, the brain's reasoning and decision-making capabilities become "off-line," leaving teenagers stuck in an emotional and sensory experience without access to logic or planning.[3] With all these impacts, trauma disrupts a person's sense of safety and predictability in this world.

Trauma can arise from various distressing incidences. While classic examples include war, torture, kidnapping, and physical or sexual assault, other situations can also be traumatic. These may include:

- surviving a serious natural disaster (e.g., flood, tornado, hurricane, earthquake, or fire)
- undergoing a serious accident (e.g., car accident, bike crash, dog bites, sports injury)
- being attacked, stabbed, shot at, or hurt badly
- seeing someone attacked, stabbed, shot at, or hurt badly
- being physically abused by family or others or seeing someone physically assaulted
- being forced or pressured to have sex
- having someone close die suddenly or violently
- being robbed
- experiencing a medical emergency (e.g., anaphylactic shock)

The severity of the event, especially if it involves serious injury or the threat of death, increases the likelihood of a traumatic response. I (Monica) am reminded of a teenager who believed that she would never feel safe again after her house was burglarized. We worked together to process her traumatic experience and to grow in knowing that the powerful presence of God through Jesus and the Holy Spirit was with her. She pressed heavily into remembering that even today she can experience the safety and refuge of God after her trauma and take practical steps of faith to face her fears. One of the practical steps the teenager took was to journal about the details of the traumatic event (including her sensory experiences—what she saw, heard, smelled, and felt). Then she read and talked about these fear-provoking details, knowing God was with her in the present moment and had brought her to safety. This practical step is exemplified in many psalms that describe in some detail the experiences of trauma and oppression (e.g., Psalm 69, 73, 77). Another practical step she took was to identify how her trauma affected the way she thought about God, other people, herself, and the world—keeping her stuck in perpetual fear. For example, prior to the trauma event, she felt safe in her home. She believed that God provided that safety. However, after the trauma event, she thought that God was telling her that she would *never* feel safe until she was in heaven. Although there is some truth to that statement, it was not completely accurate concerning the Word of God. We spent time together reflecting on and challenging that view of God through passages like Psalm 121:

> I lift up my eyes to the hills.
> From where does my help come?
> My help comes from the Lord,
> who made heaven and earth.
> He will not let your foot be moved;
> he who keeps you will not slumber.
> Behold, he who keeps Israel
> will neither slumber nor sleep.
> The Lord is your keeper;
> the Lord is your shade on your right hand.
> The sun shall not strike you by day,
> nor the moon by night.
> The Lord will keep you from all evil;
> he will keep your life.
> The Lord will keep
> your going out and your coming in
> from this time forth and forevermore.

The Gospel Amid Trauma and PTSD: The Cross of Christ as Greatest Trauma and Hope

When I (Monica) was around six years old, my younger brother died in a drowning accident during a camping trip with family and church friends. I remember that day well—the incongruity of the chaos with the bright, sunny day. This tragedy is a part of my and my family's story. We were a family who went to church, but before the accident, I did not know Jesus personally. It was during my brother's funeral service, while singing the hymn, "Nearer My God to Thee," that I came to know Jesus and accepted him as my Savior. From that day, every night, I knelt by my bed to pray to Jesus for protection and safety for our family. I came to know Jesus more and more. However, it was also after the tragedy that I began to experience symptoms of PTSD, including nightmares, flashbacks, numerous intense fears and anxieties, and consistent stomachaches, which stuck with me throughout elementary school and into my teen years. No one—not my parents, nor any other adult in my life—talked to me about how the tragedy would impact me. None of them even knew about how it was affecting me.

I share this story not out of frustration for not receiving help or having a name for what I suffered in silence, but because I hope that others will not make the same mistake and assume that a teen who has undergone a trauma is fine as long as they aren't showing any overt signs of PTSD. Additionally, when I later learned about PTSD, it was helpful to understand that my experience was a common response to suffering after a traumatic incident living in this world that is passing away.

When thinking about trauma, we don't have to read too far in the Bible to see that God's story of redemption for his people through Christ happens in the context of trauma—deep woundedness, pain, suffering, and sin—because of the fall. After the fall in Genesis, Adam and Eve experience trauma—in Genesis 4, their son

Abel is murdered, and they also lose their son Cain after he is cast out for murdering his brother. In 2 Samuel 13:1–29, Tamar is raped by her half-brother Amnon. There is national trauma in the book of Exodus as the Israelites live in slavery and violent oppression. And those are only a few examples—Scripture's redemptive narrative is densely dotted with trauma.

God does not tell his story of redemption by moving quickly to victory. He details the scope and depth of suffering, sin, and pain. In trauma, people need to cry out to God and remember him again and again, such as in Psalm 107, and to learn how to see God's redemptive work amid their traumas. Psalm 107 describes trauma befalling the people of God, whether because of their own sin or the evil of others. Repetitively interspersed throughout this Psalm are the phrases, "Then they cried to the Lord in their trouble, and he delivered them from their distress" *and* "Let them thank the Lord for his steadfast love, for his wondrous works to the children of man!" highlighting people turning back to God and faith in God's powerful redemptive work amid their traumas. In Psalm 107:33–35, we see that God is in control of this upside-down world and can make all things right:

> He turns rivers into a desert,
> springs of water into thirsty ground;
> a fruitful land into a salty waste,
> because of the evil of its inhabitants.
> He turns a desert into pools of water,
> a parched land into springs of water.

Old Testament passages like Psalm 107 exhibit the shadow of Christ, pointing Christians to the preeminent redemptive work of God through his Son Jesus. The death that Christ endured on the cross has become both the greatest place of trauma—as the Son of God took the penalty of humanity's sin—and the greatest redemptive act of God's steadfast love. Now, because of God's steadfast love through Christ, the gospel is both our present and future place of hope in trauma. Because of Jesus, we can cry out to God, and as we remember the gospel, we can be assured that God cares about the suffering and even the sin from our trauma.

This assurance that God cares about our trauma enables parents, pastors, and leaders to face the deep, dark, painful impact of trauma in teenagers' lives with hope, humility, compassion, gentleness, and courage. Because of Christ, we are not alone, whether we are teenagers suffering from trauma or we are those seeking to care for them. Christ is deeply familiar with every crevice of the valley of the shadow of death, and he fears no evil in trauma; he will indeed be the Shepherd who guides and provides.

Providing Compassionate Care: Drawing Near and Being With

Those who care for teenagers ought first to lean into the assurance, comfort, and rest found in God's completed work on the cross through Christ, even when the teenager is expressing intense fear about what happened to them in their trauma event. When we personally lean into this gospel comfort, this enables us to be strong, to be stable, and to care more compassionately for the traumatized teenager.

In this section, we provide some examples of different activities you could use to help draw out a teen suffering from trauma, who will most likely find it difficult to talk about their traumatic experience but also desperately need to do so. It is important to note that we only recommend using these activities *after* you have built a strong relationship with the teen and listened carefully to deeply understand the nature of their trauma or struggle with PTSD (for advice on how to do this effectively, see chapter 4, especially the sections on building relationships and listening carefully). Once you have done this foundational work, you can use your wisdom to select an exercise that can be helpful to them in specific ways.

Writing thoughts and feelings on leaves or clouds floating to Jesus[4]

An important way for teenagers to process their traumatic memories is to practice crying out to God. One way to help them get started with this is by using a simple activity—writing down their traumatic experience and related thoughts and feelings on leaves or clouds and then imagining them floating away to Jesus. Before a counseling session or intentional conversation, print the "Thoughts and Feelings on Leaves in a River Floating to Jesus" worksheet or the "Thoughts and Feelings: Crying Out to God" worksheet. What is key, however, is not only expressing their traumatic memories, but also learning how to cry out to God about them, since trauma survivors can get stuck in their memories. Avoidance is a feature of PTSD that may perpetuate its symptoms. Sufferers will avoid people, places, or things that remind them of the trauma. They also usually try to avoid thinking or talking about the event, but they are not able to do so completely, so they suffer from intrusive thoughts and nightmares. To intentionally think about, feel, and write down trauma memories within the context of a trusting relationship can be an important part of the healing process.

Name: ______________________________ Date: ______________

Thoughts and Feelings on Leaves in a River Floating to Jesus

Then the angel showed me the river of the water of life, bright as crystal, flowing from the throne of God and of the Lamb. (Revelation 22:1)

Name: ______________________________ Date: ______________

Thoughts and Feelings: Crying Out to God

Even before a word is on my tongue, behold, O Lord, you know it altogether. (Psalm 139:4)

4-7-8 guided breathing exercise

Teenagers who have been traumatized may experience a continual sense of threat in their bodies, even though the traumatic event is no longer occurring. They may also experience intense emotional and physiological responses to reminders of the event. Breathing exercises can slow down the heart rate to help signal to the brain and body that the threat of the trauma is no longer happening. However, as believers, we know that it is not just deep breathing that brings true comfort and calm. Rather, true peace comes through faith in the promises and presence of God through Christ and the work of the Holy Spirit. So, while we do encourage use of guided breathing exercises as a way to physiologically calm teens struggling with symptoms of PTSD, it is not a tool we recommend on its own, because it does not deal with the heart issues that are connected to the trauma experience and how the teen interprets it.

The 4-7-8 breathing exercise helps to activate relaxation through the body's nervous system. To do the breathing exercise, help the teenager get in a comfortable position. Let them know that they can either close their eyes or not—whatever helps them to be comfortable. Then guide the teenager to slowly take a deep breath in through the nose for four counts, hold their breath for seven counts, and then slowly breathe out through their mouth with pursed lips for eight counts. As they slowly breathe out, their body may start to noticeably relax. Doing this exercise together with them can be helpful so that they don't feel alone. You can do several cycles of this breathing exercise until you notice that the teenager feels calm. Here is a script you can use:

> Let's now start this breathing exercise. As we begin this exercise together, softly close your eyes. Remember that our God says in Psalm 121:2 that our help comes from the Lord, who made heaven and earth. And he can help you feel calmed as you breathe.

> Take a deep breath in through your nose for 4 counts . . . noticing your stomach expand. Now hold it for 7 counts . . . 4 . . . 5 . . . 6 . . . 7. And now slowly breathe out through your pursed lips for 8 counts . . . feeling your stomach contract . . . 7 . . . 8.
>
> Let's do this again. Breathe in through your nose . . . 3 . . . 4. Hold it . . . 2 . . . 3 . . . 4 . . . 5 . . . 6 . . . 7. Breathe out through your mouth slowly . . . noticing your shoulders dropping and relaxing . . . 7 . . . 8.
>
> Breathe in . . . 2 . . . 3 . . . 4. Hold it . . . 2 . . . 3 . . . 4 . . . 5 . . . 6 . . . 7. Breathe out slowly . . . 2 . . . 3 . . . 4 . . . 5 . . . 6 . . . 7 . . . 8.
>
> Last one . . . breathe in . . . 2 . . . 3 . . . 4. Hold it . . . 2 . . . 3 . . . 4 . . . 5 . . . 6 . . . 7. Breathe out slowly . . . allowing your arms to loosen up . . . 5 . . . 6 . . . 7 . . . 8.
>
> Now you can open your eyes.

After completing the exercise, have them reflect and discuss how this exercise went for them. Encourage them to practice this whenever they experience intrusive memories or feel on edge. Encourage them that after some deep breathing, it can be helpful to meditate on Scripture or pray.

Five senses 5-4-3-2-1 exercise

The five senses 5-4-3-2-1 activity can help the sufferer stay in the present moment, especially when they are experiencing flashbacks. Use the following descriptions to guide the teenager through this exercise:

> Name 5 things in the room God created that you can see. (Pause)

> Name 4 things God created that you can touch, and take a moment to describe what you feel with these items. (Pause)
>
> Name 3 things God created that you can hear. (Pause)
>
> Name 2 things God created that you can smell. (Pause)
>
> Now this one might be a little tricky, but describe one thing you taste in your mouth. (Pause)

After the exercise, ask them how they think they did with this and how they felt. When suffering from PTSD, we often become stuck in an internal loop of fearful thoughts and dark memories. Noticing God's creation around us can help us come out of that loop and remember where we are and who is with us. Psalm 19:1–2 says that "The heavens declare the glory of God, and the sky above proclaims his handiwork. Day to day pours out speech, and night to night reveals knowledge." God's creation declares and proclaims God's glory, which ultimately is revealed in Jesus. By staying in the present moment, the teen can remember that God is here with them now through Christ and that they can reach out to him in prayer at this very moment.

Trauma journal exercise

As mentioned previously, after a teenager experiences a traumatic event, it is not unusual for them to not want to talk about it—avoiding painful experiences, thoughts, and feelings. Avoidance strategies may provide initial relief from painful intrusive memories of trauma; however, research shows that avoiding thoughts, feelings, and conversations about the trauma can maintain or exacerbate PTSD symptoms in teenagers.[5] This journal exercise helps the teenager to face their painful experiences in a safe way before God.

Give this exercise for homework. Instruct the teenager to pick a time and place to journal—when and where they will feel comfortable and have enough time. Then before starting to write about the painful event, tell them to read and meditate on Psalm 23, about the Shepherd who leads them, our good Shepherd who is Jesus (John 10). Read it with them when giving these instructions for homework:

> The Lord is my shepherd; I shall not want.
>   He makes me lie down in green pastures.
> He leads me beside still waters.
>   He restores my soul.
> He leads me in paths of righteousness
>   for his name's sake.
>
> Even though I walk through the valley of the shadow of death,
>   I will fear no evil,
> for you are with me;
>   your rod and your staff,
>   they comfort me.
>
> You prepare a table before me
>   in the presence of my enemies;
> you anoint my head with oil;
>   my cup overflows.
> Surely goodness and mercy shall follow me
>   all the days of my life,
> and I shall dwell in the house of the Lord
>   forever.

Next, instruct them to write about the traumatic event, including as many details of the event as possible, starting out with, "Lord, this is what happened." These details should include sights they saw, sounds they heard, sensations they felt, and thoughts and feelings they had during the traumatic event. Let them know that if they are not able to write it all in one sitting, they can pause and return to complete the journaling exercise as many times as they need to until they finish telling their story. Instruct them to bring the completed exercise the next time you have another conversation with them, at which point they can read it out loud to you.

When the teen returns, first ask them how they felt about the journal exercise. Then read Psalm 23 together before having them read their full trauma account. Let them know that they can go at their pace and take their time. When they finish reading, express empathy by saying things like, "Thank you for sharing this with me," "You are really courageous to share your trauma story," or "Your pain really matters. I wish that hadn't happened to you." Then have a reflective conversation about how they felt after reading their trauma story to you. After listening, take some time to pray with them. Encourage the teenager to continue to journal to God about their trauma story as additional memories and details emerge. Also, while teenagers write, reflect on, and share their detailed trauma story, you may notice hearing some of their distorted thoughts or beliefs concerning themselves, others, and God. The next exercise will be helpful to do.

Challenging distorted thoughts/beliefs from trauma exercise

As a result of trauma, thoughts about oneself, others, the world, and God can change dramatically. This exercise helps to identify some of the distorted or inaccurate thoughts or beliefs and challenge them using biblical truths. This exercise can be done together with the teenager. On a blank piece of paper, draw a line in the middle creating two columns. The left side of the column will identify distorted thoughts or beliefs that the teenager has developed that is keeping them in a stuck loop. The right side of the column will identify biblical truths that challenge those distorted thoughts or beliefs.

When reflecting, discussing, and identifying the distorted or inaccurate thoughts or beliefs, here are a few tips to consider:

- Make sure to give the teenager time to reflect on some of the thoughts they had after the traumatic event; be quick to listen and slow to speak.
- Wonder and explore *together* about distorted thoughts or beliefs.
- Distorted thoughts or beliefs might come from the teenager's understanding of *why* the trauma happened (e.g., God let the trauma happen to teach me a lesson); ask, "Hmm . . . why do *you* think this event happened?"
- Distorted thoughts or beliefs may contain some truth but will not be fully accurate.
- Distorted thoughts or beliefs can often be identified in an "If, then" structure (e.g., "If I wasn't late, then this wouldn't have happened to the family").
- Distorted thoughts or beliefs often use extreme language, such as "never" and "always" (e.g., "I will *never* be safe until I am in heaven").

Developing healthy sleeping habits

As embodied souls, it is common to have sleep issues after experiencing trauma. However, developing healthy sleep habits, which includes quality and quantity of sleep, will help with healing from the effects of trauma.[6] So, talking to the teenager about their sleep habits and jointly exploring and developing a plan for good sleep will be loving and wise. In general, to build good sleep habits, it is important to create a consistent, calming bedtime routine, which often includes ending the use of electronic screens at least thirty minutes before sleep.[7] Regular exercise and healthy eating will also help with better sleep. It's important to help teens who struggle to sleep after trauma to remember that they can find ultimate rest for their body, mind, and soul because of the grace of God through Jesus. Our "help comes from the Lord, who made heaven and earth. He will not let your foot be moved; he who keeps you will not slumber" (Psalm 121:2–3).

Warning Signs for When Additional Help Is Needed

As you care for teenagers who have experienced trauma, you might be wondering at what point they might need additional help. As mentioned previously, many teenagers who have gone through trauma may not develop PTSD. However, while you draw near to them in their trauma and intentionally care for them, there are some warning signs that additional help is needed after you have walked alongside them for more than three months:

- The teenager still has nightmares about the event(s).
- The teenager has intrusive thoughts, memories, or images about the event when they do not want to have them.
- The teenager is still intentionally avoiding places or situations that remind them of the traumatic event or trying hard not to think about the event.
- The teenager is still feeling on guard or easily startled.
- The teenager is feeling numb or detached from people, activities, or their surroundings.
- The teenager is increasingly angry or aggressive.
- The teenager continues to feel guilt or shame or is unable to stop blaming themselves or others for the traumatic event.

If you are a parent, this increased circle of care and support might involve going to the pediatrician with your teen to talk about their symptoms and experiences. It might involve reaching out to schoolteachers and school counselors to see how they can be supportive of your teen while they are at school. It might mean helping them receive formal counseling from a mental health professional.

God Holds Our Hands

After teenagers experience trauma, they can additionally continue to experience pain and suffering. They may feel like they are living in constant fear. But Scripture reminds us that the Lord our God has taken hold of our right hand and says, "Do not fear; I will help you" (Isaiah 41:13). May we as parents, pastors, and youth leaders walk with our teenagers in their trauma, holding their hands closely, remembering and believing that our God drew near to us through the incarnation of his son, Jesus, and is the One who helps them and is with them in their fright.

CHAPTER 12

Teenagers with Schizophrenia or Bipolar Disorder

A few months before his freshman year, Frank began to isolate himself in his room, becoming very withdrawn from his family and friends. This was not too alarming for the family since he was generally a quiet boy. Then around his freshman year in high school, there were more obvious changes in his behavior. He began to isolate himself more and more each day, staying alone in his room. Frank's parents didn't know what he did in his room, but he seemed more and more out of reach and out of touch. His mom would try to talk with him, and when he did talk, it was about matters that were disconnected with what was going on in the present or what was happening around him. Sometimes he would talk about seeing things that she could not see, such as God, who he claimed also gave him the power to see these images around him, like fire. Sometimes he would start talking only to suddenly stop, seemingly frozen. He was physically present but seemed mentally absent, his body still with his eyes staring blankly. His high school teachers and administrators began to reach out because they noticed that even though he attended class, he was not engaged, and he was unable to complete his classwork or be involved in classroom discussions. The school psychologist diagnosed Frank with schizophrenia.

Over our twenty-nine years in ministry, we have cared for teenagers who suffered from schizophrenia and bipolar disorder, two of the most ominous sounding conditions, especially to someone with little or no formal training in mental health or counseling. When someone suffering from schizophrenia or bipolar comes into the church, it can be difficult for people to know how to respond. At times, people blatantly stay away from those suffering from these conditions, usually because they are extremely uncomfortable. This was sometimes my (Danny's) or our church's reaction.

Sometimes these more extreme mental health conditions presented themselves in the form of a teenager's strange mutterings, sudden absence from church for long periods, or verbal outbursts during a Bible study. We have also sat alongside caregivers at meetings with their mental health professionals or a school psychologist when the caregiver first learned that their teenager has schizophrenia or bipolar disorder. Ultimately, the reality of these more difficult mental health issues needs to be discussed and understood by parents, pastors, and youth leaders in our churches. Although they occur less frequently than some of the other conditions discussed in this book, they are present and can significantly impact teens and their families. Love enriched by deeper understanding will help us wisely care for both caregivers and their teenagers.

Although schizophrenia is distinct from bipolar disorder, we decided to address these two conditions together in this chapter since there is some similar practical help that is essential for both disorders.

Understanding Schizophrenia

The following features characterize schizophrenia:[1]

- Delusions: Believing something is true even though there is evidence to show otherwise. Delusions can include a variety of themes (e.g., believing someone is out to get them, believing that a stranger or a famous person who does not know them is in love with them, feeling that they have a serious illness without proof, having distorted religious ideas like they are God, or believing they are extremely powerful).

- Hallucinations: Vividly and clearly seeing or hearing things that others do not see or hear.
- Disorganized thinking or speech.
- Grossly disorganized or abnormal motor behavior (including catatonia—when a person seems to be frozen).
- Negative symptoms (e.g., diminished emotional expression or decrease in self-initiated purposeful activities).

To receive a diagnosis of schizophrenia from a qualified mental health professional, two or more of the above features must be present for a significant portion of time and persist for at least six months. In addition, there also must be an impairment in the level of functioning in one or more areas, such as work, social relations, or self-care.

While schizophrenia can develop during adolescence, the incidence during the teen years is very low. Even among adults, this condition is very uncommon; its highest incidence rate is 1 percent among adults. The average onset of schizophrenia is eighteen to twenty-five years for males and twenty-three to thirty-five years for women.[2] Although research identifies various intersecting factors (e.g., biology, heritability, and environment) that are linked to schizophrenia, a study by Cardno and Gottesman suggests that more than 80 percent of the risk of developing schizophrenia is due to genetics.[3]

Schizophrenia is generally a chronic illness, which often requires extensive help from family and other sources (e.g., long-term inpatient treatment). Still, the sooner medical treatment is sought, the better stabilization could be.[4] According to the American Academy of Child and Adolescent Psychiatry, there is a high risk of relapse if psychiatric medication is discontinued.[5] Furthermore, research shows that high levels of expressed emotion in the family (i.e., hostility, emotional overinvolvement, and criticism) can worsen the teenager's suffering from schizophrenia.[6] Awareness of this kind of information can help parents, pastors, and other church leaders to compassionately care for the teenager who is affected while trying to make sense of and navigate this illness.

Understanding Bipolar Disorder

Bipolar disorder is characterized by periods of intense emotional states (i.e., manic/hypomanic, and depressive) that affect a person's mood, energy, and ability to function.[7] These periods, called mood episodes, can last from days to weeks and are present nearly every day for most of the day. Manic/hypomanic episodes can include three or more of the following:

- Grandiosity
- Decreased need for sleep
- More talkative than usual or pressure to keep talking
- Flight of ideas or subjective experience of racing thoughts
- Distractibility
- An increase in goal-directed activity or psychomotor agitation
- Excessive involvement in activities that have painful consequences (e.g., unrestrained buying sprees or inappropriate sexual behaviors)

Depressive episodes involve a deeply sad mood or a loss of the ability to feel joy or pleasure. Though mood swings can occur in individuals without bipolar disorder, these changes are generally shorter, lasting hours instead of days, and don't usually come with drastic shifts in behavior or significant disruptions in daily life, such as challenges with routines or social interactions. Bipolar disorder, on the other hand, can strain personal relationships and make it hard to maintain work or school responsibilities.

Bipolar disorder can start in adolescence, with 59 percent of adults with the condition recalling symptoms during childhood or adolescence.[8] Research indicates that approximately 1 percent of teenagers are affected by bipolar.[9] However, bipolar disorder usually is diagnosed between the ages of twenty and thirty; males may develop it slightly earlier than females.[10] Studies show that bipolar disorder is a long-term condition, especially for those with early onset (i.e., onset under eighteen years of age).[11] Once it starts, people typically experience cycles of manic and depressive episodes throughout their lives. Over time, these episodes can become more frequent, especially if not treated.[12]

The way bipolar disorder shows up can differ by age, but in teenagers it is fairly similar to how it manifests in adults, with symptoms like elevated mood, grandiosity, paranoia, and rapid flight of ideas. Bipolar disorder significantly impacts many aspects of life, including both academic challenges and trouble with friendships or family relationships. During manic or depressive episodes, teenagers can struggle to function normally.

Bipolar disorder tends to run in families, and genetics plays a strong role.[13] Because diagnosing bipolar disorder in teenagers is complex and often difficult, with many of the symptoms overlapping with other conditions like ADHD, PTSD, depression, and anxiety, it is important to seek professional help from a trusted psychiatrist if you suspect a teen under your care has bipolar disorder.

In adults with bipolar disorder, a delay in receiving treatment can lead to worse outcomes, including increased hospitalizations and a higher risk of suicide attempts.[14] Although there is limited data on this aspect of bipolar disorder in adolescents, it is suspected that untreated symptoms in youth can have similar negative effects. Medications will play a central role in managing bipolar disorder.[15] According to the American Academy of Child and Adolescent Psychiatry, a combination of medication and psychotherapy is recommended for teenagers with bipolar disorder. Medication can help to regulate mood, reduce the severity and frequency of manic and depressive episodes, and improve overall functioning and quality of life. Early intervention with medication can also help prevent long-term complications associated with untreated bipolar disorder.[16] Both the teenager who is struggling with bipolar disorder and their family must understand the risks (e.g., more severe course of the illness and hospitalization) of not getting treatment (i.e., medication and therapy).[17]

The Gospel Amid Schizophrenia and Bipolar Disorder: Looking to Our Compassionate Savior

Schizophrenia and bipolar disorder are complex conditions that are difficult to understand and wisely respond to. Over the years, when I (Danny) have had students with these struggles, I have at times felt bewildered, frustrated, and hopeless. If this is your experience, it is important to remember that we can always express compassion, and that doing so can bring deep peace to ourselves and to the teen under our care. Matthew 14:14 says that when Jesus "went ashore he saw a great crowd, and he had compassion on them and healed their sick." This is just one of many places where Jesus's compassion is noted throughout the Gospels. Jesus was often moved to compassion because he saw people as helpless and like sheep without a shepherd. Whether a parent or a church leader, having a gospel heart of compassion in these difficult and complex struggles can be an anchor for the teen and their family.

As we reflect upon the compassion Jesus had for the sick, his gospel reminds us that we ourselves—parents, pastors, and youth leaders—had been sick beyond ability to heal ourselves. But because of God's great compassion through Jesus, "who for the joy that was set before him endured the cross, despising the shame, and is seated at the right hand of the throne of God" (Hebrews 12:2), we now have been healed of our gravest sickness and reconciled to God. So, now we look to Jesus, through whom we are called to clothe ourselves with "compassionate hearts, kindness, humility, meekness, and patience" (Colossians 3:12) to care for teenagers with schizophrenia or bipolar.

These qualities are essential. Being compassionate, kind, humble, meek, and patient will involve listening well and not confronting the struggling teenager with their delusions directly but kindly suggesting a different perspective. Once, the two of us took a teenager (diagnosed with bipolar and schizophrenia) out for lunch, and as we listened, she talked furiously about how God was very angry at her and was out get her. We empathized with her experience and expressed how scary that must be. We listened some more, asking a few questions to know more about how she felt. We asked her if she would like to hear a different perspective, and when she indicated that she would, we shared about the steadfast love of God that endures for her, expressed in a short verse like Psalm 136:1. Then we enjoyed each other's company and the Chick-fil-A meal together.

Providing Compassionate Care: Drawing Near and Being With

Schizophrenia and bipolar disorders are complex. Family counseling and individual counseling are key strategies to help teenagers and their families. Family counseling is especially valuable in the early stages of teenagers who suffer with bipolar disorder and schizophrenia, as it provides education to teenagers and their families about their condition and helps them recognize triggers and early symptoms. It also helps families reduce criticism and emotional tension, which can exacerbate their teen's struggles. The complexities of schizophrenia and bipolar disorder will lead most churches to focus on providing supportive care for the family and teenager, rather than facilitating the family's counseling. These include finding practical ways to support and love the teenager at church and meeting up with the teenager to especially talk about their faith and who God is amid their struggles.

One of the ways we have done this is to offer an open line of communication through texting with the teen. This gives them a forum where they can text, when they feel comfortable. We recall one student who at first was not very responsive in person but later, through text, suddenly began sharing very intimate and profound questions about herself, her struggles, and her faith. These back-and-forth exchanges across a few days eventually provided an opportunity to meet up and talk in person. Finally, after she felt more comfort and stability with us, we encouraged her to get involved in the youth group more actively, and we asked some peers to invest in her. It was amazing to see how she went from feeling like a loner to feeling a place of love and warmth at church.

When we are ministering to the families of teens with schizophrenia or bipolar disorder, the concept of expressed emotion, which we introduced and discussed in more detail in chapter 4, is important to emphasize here. As a reminder, expressed emotion is a measure of how people spontaneously talk about or react to those with a mental illness. While expressed emotion specifically measures three to five aspects of the social context, the most important are critical comments, hostility, and emotional overinvolvement. Studies have shown that a high level of expressed emotion in the home and other relationship dynamics (i.e., hostility, emotional overinvolvement, and criticism) can worsen the recovery in patients with mental illness.[18] Here are some examples of expressed emotion that studies have found: When those who are unable to get up in the morning, who fail to wash regularly, or who do not do household tasks are criticized for being lazy and selfish; when parents or caregivers get angry or irritated; when those with schizophrenia are told they are causing a lot of problems for the family; or when there is excessive sacrifice or overprotectiveness.[19] The negative effects of this treatment are not surprising, since Scripture specifically warns against harshness and provocation in our relationships with our children; for example, Colossians 3:21 says, "Fathers, do not provoke your children, lest they become discouraged." Helping parents become aware of the call to not show hostility or continually criticize a struggling teen is an important way we can care for teens and their families. Instead, we can encourage the teen's caregivers to pursue being gentle, warm, and kind in their conversations.

Here are some recommendations for how you can respond when the teenager starts talking about their hallucinations/delusions:[20]

- Listen and reflect. Let them know what you've heard from them by simply repeating what they've said. (e.g., "So God spoke to you and was terrorizing you.")
- Be respectful and take a rational approach based on facts. (e. g., If your teenager says, "The neighbor is spying on me for the government," you can respond with, "I'm really sorry you're going through that—it sounds scary and stressful. I haven't noticed anything like that myself, but I believe you're really feeling it. I'm here for you, and we can figure this out together.")
- Don't agree with or reinforce their hallucinations or delusions. (e. g., "You're totally right!" or "I see what you're seeing.")
- Avoid direct confrontation of hallucinations/delusions (e.g., "That's impossible. Stop thinking that!" "That's not true!").
- Suggest a different perspective. (e. g, If your teenager says, "The voices on the television are talking directly to me. They're sending me secret messages," you can respond with, "I can see that feels very real to you, and I'm not here to argue with what you're experiencing. I haven't heard those messages myself, though, and from what I understand, television shows usually just televise a show for everyone.")
- Empathize on what you can agree on. You might not agree on the specific delusion or hallucination, but you can agree on the feelings that are behind them. (e. g., "That sounds really stressful," "You must feel really frightened and unsafe.").

- Offer empathy when disagreeing (e. g., "It's hard for me to see that you're being threatened because I can't hear the voices. But that sounds very stressful!").
- Avoid forcefulness in your response. Avoid getting into arguments or pushing a teenager into insight on their illness. This may lead to depression and increased suicide risk.
- Be mindful of not creating too much stress by developing low-stress routines in the home that they can do at their pace.
- Offer your teen space to calm down.

Warning Signs for When Additional Help Is Needed

The following warning signs may help you know when to reach out to a professional regarding your teen's struggle with schizophrenia:[21]

- Changes in the way a person thinks, acts, and experiences the world
- Delusions (e.g., misattribute threatening intent to an innocuous comment; experience family members or friends as being unfamiliar, leading to the delusional belief that they have been replaced by an alien)
- Hallucinations (e.g., hearing voices that others do not hear)
- Incoherent thoughts and speech patterns (e.g., stop talking in the middle of a thought, jump from topic to topic, or make up words that have no meaning)
- Deteriorations in social relationships, academic performance, and personal hygiene
- Isolations from family and friends
- Diminished emotional expression and speech
- Low energy and spending a lot of time in passive activities

According to the National Institute of Mental Health, the following are some warning signs for bipolar disorder in teens, which may help know when to reach out to a professional:[22]

Common signs and symptoms of mania:
- Showing intense happiness or silliness
- Having a very short temper or seeming extremely irritable
- Talking very fast or having racing thoughts
- Having an inflated sense of ability, knowledge, and power
- Doing reckless things that show poor judgment

Common signs and symptoms of depression:
- Feeling very sad or hopeless
- Feeling lonely or isolating from others
- Eating too much or too little
- Having little energy and no interest in usual activities
- Sleeping too much

If you are a parent, increasing your circle of care and support might involve going to the pediatrician with your teen to discuss their symptoms and experiences and your concerns for them. It might involve reaching out to schoolteachers and school counselors to see how they can be supportive for the struggling teen while they are at school. It might mean your teen receiving formal counseling from a mental health professional.

For treatment of teenagers with bipolar disorder and schizophrenia, a well-established treatment is known as family focused therapy (FFT),[23] which is a multimodal treatment approach that includes family involvement. The family is taught about the illness (i.e., symptoms, course of the illness, and medications), as well as how to support their teenager who suffers with the illness. Learning how to support their teenager may involve both the family and teenager building skills together (i.e., communication, problem-solving, and emotion regulation skills).[24] Studies show that improved parenting skills, family flexibility, and family positive reframing has been linked to improved mood and functioning in teenagers with bipolar disorder.[25]

Children of God

Schizophrenia or bipolar disorder might be the struggle a teenager faces, but it does not define them. It might be what they have, but it is not who they are. As parents, pastors, and youth leaders, we have a wonderful calling to help teenagers and their families see that they are greater than their schizophrenia and bipolar disorder. John 1:12 states that those who believe in Christ are the children of God. No mental illness can change this truth.

CHAPTER 13

Teenagers with Suicidal Ideation

No matter how long you've been in ministry, nothing prepares you for when a student says they want to take their own life. It's always shocking and frightening. One of the most vivid stories we can recall is of a student who was having trouble with his girlfriend, because her parents forbade their relationship, once they found out. The girlfriend's parents made sure that they would not talk or see each other at all, even though both teenagers expressed still loving each other. This spiraled the teenage boy into great distress. In fact, he was so distressed that he created a specific plan—at a certain time and place, he would step out onto the road near a busy intersection and take his own life. He wrote about his plans and secretly messaged this to his girlfriend, who subsequently told us about them. We intervened and compassionately and gently talked to the teenager.

Other times, these situations might not be as dramatic, and yet hearing a student say they want to "kill themselves" is still scary and extremely worrisome. We have known numerous teenagers over the years who have faced various levels of depression and shared that they wanted to end their life. It is never easy to hear, and we take these words very seriously.

Unlike the other chapters so far in Part 2, this chapter's focus is not a mental health disorder. However, we chose to give suicidal ideation a chapter of its own because it commonly co-occurs with a wide variety of mental health illnesses, including mood disorders (e.g., depression and bipolar), severe anxiety, eating disorders, substance abuse, and personality disorders. According to SAMHSA's 2023 data, 12.3 percent of teenagers aged twelve to seventeen had serious thoughts of suicide in the past year; 5.6 percent of teenagers made a suicide plan; and 3.3 percent of teenagers attempted suicide in the past year.[1] Teenage females are six to nine times more likely to attempt suicide, but teenage males are five times more likely to die by suicide.[2] Since 2007, the suicide rate among ten to twenty-four-year-olds in the US has risen significantly, increasing by approximately 57 percent between 2007 and 2018.[3] The ten- to twenty-four-year-old age group accounts for 15 percent of all suicides.[4] While the suicide rate for this age group is lower than for other groups, suicide is the second leading cause of death in this age group.[5]

Suicide is influenced by a range of factors, including chronic or terminal illness, family history of suicide or mental illness, media exposure with suicide content (which can lead to suicide contagion or copycat behavior), physical or sexual abuse, previous suicide attempts, peer victimization, and access to lethal means.[6] To help prevent suicide, it is important to be aware of the warning signs of suicidal intent; this list by NAMI is a helpful one to become familiar with. People with suicidal intent are marked by:[7]

- Giving away personal possessions
- Talking as if they're saying goodbye or going away forever
- Taking steps to tie up loose ends
- Stockpiling pills or obtaining a weapon
- Preoccupation with death
- Sudden cheerfulness or calm after a period of despondency
- Dramatic changes in personality, mood and/or behavior
- Increased drug or alcohol use
- Saying things like "Nothing matters anymore," "You'll be better off without me," or "Life isn't worth living"
- Withdrawal from friends, family, and normal activities
- Failed romantic relationship

- Sense of utter hopelessness and helplessness
- History of suicide attempts or other self-harming behaviors
- History of family/friend suicide or attempts

In particular, it's important to know that more than 90 percent of teenagers who died by suicide had a psychiatric diagnosis, particularly depression,[8] so it's important to be especially attuned to these signs in teens with a diagnosed mental illness.

The Gospel Amid Suicidal Ideation: A Better Way Out

In Philippians 1:22–24, Paul expresses the anguish, sorrow, and pain he experienced while imprisoned:

> If I am to live in the flesh, that means fruitful labor for me. Yet which I shall choose I cannot tell. I am hard pressed between the two. My desire is to depart and be with Christ, for that is far better. But to remain in the flesh is more necessary on your account.

Whether or not Paul is referencing suicide in this passage, we do know that while he was in anguish, he desired to die and be with Christ. Christians, like Paul, can feel various kinds of anguish that leads to the desire to die. While living in this world full of suffering, suicide is a common way people, including teenagers, seek to bring an end to their suffering.

However, the Bible is very clear that each life is precious. Genesis 1:27 speaks to how God created people in his image; Psalm 139:13–14 emphasizes how God knits us together in the womb and praises God for how we are fearfully and wonderfully made; and Matthew 10:29–31 says that all the hairs on our head are numbered and that we are more valuable than sparrows. God cares for our lives intimately. If we are in Christ, we are a temple of God in which the Holy Spirit dwells (1 Corinthians 6:19–20). There are so many passages that show how precious our lives are to God. Perhaps the ultimate expression of how precious we are to God is John 3:16, which says, "For God so loved the world, that he gave his only Son, that whoever believes in him should not perish but have eternal life." God cares for people he has made in his image so much that he willingly gave his own Son to rescue them (Romans 8:32).

Knowing that our lives are precious to God can give teenagers important reasons to live when they are thinking about suicide. It can also encourage teenagers to see how their lives are precious to other people around them even though their pain says otherwise. Our aim is to help teenagers continue to persevere grasping onto the hopes and promises of God that one day there will be relief from all our pain.

Now returning to the passage in Philippians, Paul found an important reason to "live in the flesh." In verses 24–26, Paul says,

> But to remain in the flesh is more necessary on your account. Convinced of this, I know that I will remain and continue with you all, for your progress and joy in the faith, so that in me you may have ample cause to glory in Christ Jesus, because of my coming to you again.

Paul remained "in the flesh" for the people of God and their progress and joy in the faith. We can lovingly shepherd the students in our care to embrace the good purpose God has for their lives here and now.

Providing Compassionate Care: Drawing Near and Being With

Those who care for teenagers with suicidal ideation ought first to lean into the assurance, comfort, and rest found in God's completed work on the cross through Christ, even when the teenager shares thoughts about harming themselves. When we personally lean into this gospel comfort, it enables us to be strong, to be stable, and to care more compassionately for the teenager. In this section, we provide some tools to help a teen struggling with suicidal thoughts.

There are ways in which a church and youth ministry can be protective against suicide. A teenager's faith can provide hope in the midst of suicidal ideation, and their church community can help them learn how to press into God's truth of who they are in Christ in the midst of the suffering that is leading them to consider suicide as a way out. The gospel offers a sense of belonging that can be critical, depending on the nature of the teen's suffering. Other protective factors against suicide include a teenager's perception of strong family connections, good academic performance, positive peer relationships, impulse control, and access to mental health care. For parents, pastors, and church leaders, gaining awareness of the risk factors and protective factors for suicide is an important first step in loving and caring for teenagers who are in anguish.

Using a tool to assess suicide risk

The Columbia-Suicide Severity Rating Scale (C-SSRS)[9] is a short, practical assessment tool that has been validated by research. Pastors, parents, and youth leaders can use the C-SSRS to help identify the teenager's risk for suicide, particularly if they're not sure whether the teen has thought about suicide or if they're unsure whether or not the teen needs immediate help. This tool is free and accessible for any person or organization to use. On the Columbia Lighthouse Project's website, they state that training or experience is not necessary to use the C-SSRS, but they do provide further training in suicide prevention for those who desire to become better equipped. It is important to note that the C-SSRS is not a diagnostic tool, but it is simply a guided way to ask difficult questions about suicidal intent and help you gain clearer understanding if additional help is needed, and if so, what kind. There is also a downloadable smartphone app that is very easy to use and guides any parent, pastor, and leader to ask the necessary questions. This version will ask if you would like to share your location so that should the teenager need to go to the hospital, local resources would be provided.

To use this tool well as a parent, pastor, or youth leader, it is important to identify, ahead of your conversation with the teen, what steps you will take after gaining some insight into their level of suicide risk. Although the C-SSRS provides a general understanding of what you should do next if the teen is at low, moderate, or high risk of suicide, it is important to identify how you will specifically take those steps. For example, if they're at moderate risk for suicide, what counselor or counseling organization will you refer them to? If they're at high risk, will you call 911 or escort them to the hospital yourself? Which hospital? Or would you call the National Suicide Prevention Lifeline at 988 first? If you are not their parent, how and when will parents be contacted? These and many other questions should be considered before you ask the questions in the C-SSRS so that you are prepared to take action.

Safety planning together

In addition to using the C-SSRS, we can help a teenager develop a safety plan. If the teen has expressed any thoughts about suicide or wished that they were dead, but do not have some of the more serious risk factors, we should still help them develop a safety plan. A safety plan is not contractual in any legal sense. It is simply a written list of strategies and sources of support that teenagers can use before or during a crisis. The goal of this plan is to provide structure and ways to access help when they are struggling with suicidal thoughts.

The plan can include strategies for how to respond to suicidal thoughts with wisdom and gospel hope, along with identifying important supports such as people to contact when they're in crisis. An important component of a Christian's safety plan is reminders of the powerful and unchanging promises of God. Strategies might include praying, reading a particular passage in the Bible, relaxation exercises, physical activities, mental exercises, and enjoyable activities. Importantly, safety plans should include steps to remove access to potential means of suicide, such as locking up weapons and medications. The plan should be easily accessible and include clear instructions on what to do in case of an emergency. A helpful resource is a free app called Suicide Safety Plan, which gives teenager easy access to their plan on their phone.[10]

What else can parents and churches do?

The C-SSRS tool can also be used by teenagers for their friends who might be struggling with suicidal thoughts. As a church, you might develop a training program for teenagers who are interested in doing peer-to-peer ministry, giving them the opportunity to care for peers who are struggling with suicidal ideation.

Other resources on Columbia Lighthouse Project's website could be used to further help the church or youth ministry. Brochures can be printed and made available in churches or youth ministry rooms.[11]

In cases of helping teenagers and their families in the aftermath of a suicide attempt, it would be important and helpful, with the family and teenager's permission, to do visitations in the hospital from the church, including youth leaders and perhaps a few peer friends. Likewise, as far as a youth ministry, it could be beneficial to have a peer group of friends intentionally welcome the teenager back to the youth group after a suicide attempt, as long as this respects the confidentially of the teenager and is done only with their and their family's permission.

Finally, if there are teenagers who have lost a family member or friend to suicide, it is important to follow up with them. We knew teenagers who lost family members to suicide, as well as classmates in school. In these cases, it is important to follow up by offering times to talk and process with the student. This is not just a one-time thing but can happen over time; you want to repeatedly check in, ask how the student is doing, and see if they want to meet and talk.

One Body in Christ

Suicidal ideation means teenagers are in a dark and difficult place. They can feel alone and hopeless. As parents, pastors, and youth leaders, it might be a difficult task, but we are called to bring the hope of the gospel to them, which gives them purpose for living. This might not be an easy task. But we have a calling to be connected and stay connected with teenagers, as we are all members in one body together, as Romans 12:5 reminds us—"so we, though many, are one body in Christ, and individually members one of another." Let's bring the hope of the gospel and healing to our teenagers struggling with suicidal ideation, as one body in Christ.

CHAPTER 14

Teenagers with Excessive Screen Use Issues

In our broader culture, the impact of screen use and social media consumption is becoming a greater concern. The 2024 US Surgeon General's Advisory on the Mental Health & Well-Being of Parents stated that 70 percent of parents say parenting is more difficult than it was twenty years ago, with a child's use of technology and social media cited as the top two reasons.[1] Similarly, a majority of parents and caregivers of adolescents say they were concerned that their child's use of social media could lead to problems with anxiety or depression, self-esteem, being harassed or bullied by others, feeling pressured to act a certain way, and exposure to explicit content.[2] While social media use and even addiction to it is not categorized as a mental illness, evidence of its negative impact on teen mental health has become so clear that it cannot be ignored. Hence, this chapter will be different in format than the prior chapters of Part 2.

Because many parents today grew up without the onslaught of screen use and social media, we really struggle to comprehend how much stress and anxiety it places on our children. For example, we were surprised when I (Danny) once took an innocent picture of our teenagers playing Nintendo Switch together during their winter break. I subsequently posted this on social media, in what I thought was a touching picture of siblings bonding together through gaming. But we were surprised when one of them came to us upset that Danny had posted the picture because he was in a raggy T-shirt and looked like he just rolled out of bed. He didn't like his appearance, and he was upset that the whole world would be seeing it. In fact, he was so distraught that I (Danny) immediately took the picture down and apologized to him. Little did we know the power of social media and how important it was for him to look a certain way.

Many families will share the difficulties they have with their teenagers about their level of screen use and the amount of social media they consume. Researchers such as Jonathan Haidt and Jean Twenge have been writing about the detrimental impact that social media use has had on the lives of teenagers. The Netflix show *The Social Dilemma* also provides a look into the impact that social media has on the lives of teenagers. Numerous other studies have also stated that internet addiction is a disorder that is "the compulsive and problematic use of the internet, resulting in significant functional impairment in several life domains."[3]

Another National Institute of Health study considered whether internet addiction should be listed in the DSM. It stated that internet addiction shows "the features of excessive use, withdrawal phenomena, tolerance, and negative repercussions that characterize many substance use disorders."[4] Many are also predicting that students' continual screen use and social media consumption will likely be the leading factor in their mental health long-term. Related to this, Jean Twenge writes, "If Gen Alpha continues the Gen Z trend of being engulfed in the social media maelstrom at young ages, they may also continue the trend toward more depression and self-harm among tweens and teens."[5] Similarly, a surgeon general study found that teenagers who spend more than three hours a day on their screen also face double the risk of mental health problems, including experiencing symptoms of depression and anxiety.[6] This is concerning, as a recent survey showed that teenagers spend an average of three and a half hours a day on social media.[7] And when asked about the impact of social media on their body image, 46 percent of adolescents aged thirteen to seventeen said social media makes them feel worse.[8]

In addition to this, many social media platforms are designed to be addictive. This is because of the business model adopted by social media companies; many social media apps are free to use, but the companies that run them then find other ways to make money. The most common way, usually detailed in terms of service agreements, is for the social media platform to collect and sell user data to advertisers. The longer somebody uses a social media app, the more data there is to sell. Additionally, spending more time on social media means advertisers have more opportunities to reach you. Likewise, they can get you to increase the time you use social media, cause you to forgo social activities and personal interactions, and make it difficult for you to reduce your time using them.

The Gospel Amid Excessive Screen Use: Filling Our Hearts with What Is Beneficial

Obviously, when the Bible was written, no one had social media, computers, or smartphones. However, the Bible does speak directly to the harm or benefit of things we intake as God's creatures. Proverbs 4:23 says, "Keep your heart with all vigilance, for from it flow the springs of life." Philippians 4:8 says, "Finally, brothers, whatever is true, whatever is honorable, whatever is just, whatever is pure, whatever is lovely, whatever is commendable, if there is any excellence, if there is anything worthy of praise, think about these things." These verses speak to the importance of guarding our hearts and minds and filling them with beneficial and not harmful things.

Teenagers will often seek out social media and video games to feel known and connected to others or to feel powerful in some way. We can remind them that (1) God knows them and gave Jesus to die for them; (2) in Christ, they have the community of the church; and (3) in the case of believing teenagers, God has given them a purpose and mission to fulfill as part of his kingdom. As we invite teenagers into the community of the local church, we can give them opportunities to experience all of these realities of the gospel.

Providing Compassionate Care: Churches and Parents Walking Together

In our experience, many people serving in churches and youth ministries often state how much phones are a distraction to their small groups and Bible studies. Even teenagers at church youth retreats, lock-ins, or overnight mission trips can't sleep without their phones, and many of them are on their phones continuously, both during events as well as during their free time. In a recent study done by Pew Research, 72 percent of high school teachers say phones are a major distraction in the classroom.[9] Hence, in schools and educational settings, similar to churches, many teachers say smartphone distraction is a major issue, and more recently, many states are mounting government efforts to crack down on rampant student phone use. At the heart of this issue is care for teenagers and the negative impact of excessive screen use has.

So, if screen use and social media use is so potentially harmful to teenagers, how can the church and youth ministries help and walk with parents and teenagers? Here are some suggestions for ways churches can serve parents and caregivers in dealing with excessive screen use and the accompanying worries and stressors:

1. **For parents, foster open dialogue, conversation, and learning spaces about parental stress and social media use.** This book is not only about teenagers and mental health and how the church and youth ministries can serve them, but also about their parents and caregivers and how the church must be aware and be able to help and serve them as well. Offering care and counseling for parents and caregivers is a way for churches to serve them, especially considering how social media and

technology is a daily stressor in their lives. This serving and equipping includes offering learning spaces for caregivers about topics related to social media use. It's important to help parents and caregivers in your church understand the impact of phone and social media use, as well as understand and even determine age-appropriate recommendations for when to provide phones for their children. Likewise, understanding the potential hazards of social media use is also important for parents and caregivers.

2. **Provide parents and caregivers with resources to address parental stressors and help them connect to crucial support services.** Just as we suggest the church develop a solid list of mental health services and provider options for teenagers, the same should be true for parents in your church. This could be as simple as churches offering parent support groups, prayer groups, or even pastoral care and visitations, workshops, and Bible studies for parents and caregivers. This could also mean offering solid options for outside counseling and support in their community. Our local school district often has speakers come to talk to parents about social media, and the parents of our youth ministry always appreciate it when I kept them informed of these community events. Likewise, when a good program on television about teenage social media use would be coming on, I would also inform parents of these shows so they could be better resourced and supported.
3. **Create opportunities for connections among parents and caregivers to support one another.** Parents and caregivers can also serve and be cared for by a Sunday school class, an evening gathering/support group during youth group, or a regular prayer meeting. The church can act as a catalyst to mobilize and support parents so they can foster support and care for each other.

Navigating screen use in the home

Parents, you might need to consider ways to curb screen time use in your teenagers, which churches and youth ministries can also help with. Families can create a family media plan to help establish healthy technology boundaries at home—including screen time and social media use. In our ministry to families and teenagers over the years, we understand that there are often differences in how adults and teenagers see things, which can subsequently cause disagreement and even strife between them. Moreover, in the case of screen time, social media, and technology use, teenagers often might see their friends' households have much looser limits or no boundaries with cell phones, computers, or social media use, so they might think it unfair when comparing it with their home. As a church and youth ministry, we are aware of this dynamic and have often had to help caregivers and teenagers work through these issues. One thing we have done as a church is meet the adults and teenagers as a family, help them listen to one another, and serve as a mediator or "negotiator" to help foster a good social media plan in their household. Parents, do not be afraid to ask a youth leader or pastor from your church to serve in this role for your family. Whether you're a parent or a church leader working with parents, here are some important tips to consider when creating a family social media plan:

1. Help families create clear expectations within their families. This most likely means clearly and even physically writing down their plan. This is not to serve as a blood covenant or contract with penalties, but it can be an evolving document that the family continues to add to or subtract from. But most importantly, it can serve as a mutually agreed upon list of expectations that can be referenced by all family members.

Parents, you might even be surprised, especially due to generational differences, by all the issues that come with this. It is important to prepare yourselves and know this is an evolving document.

We can tell you that we were not ready for our teenagers to tell us they needed their phones by their bedside for alarm clocks in the morning. It seemed like a totally important need, but one which would potentially permit them to have their phones by their bedside all night. These small, minute, or informal details are important as part of one's family plan, even if they're not easy.

2. Teach teenagers about technology use. Teaching teenagers in your church about technology and empowering them to be responsible with it can be an important task of the church and youth ministry, and a way churches can walk alongside parents. This includes starting with creating tech-free zones at the youth group and encouraging teenagers to foster in-person friendships. This might include small groups and Bible studies on technology and social media use. While the church and youth ministry are not the parents, we can walk alongside parents and caregivers and guide teenagers with screen and social media use. We can help disciple them in the ways that their social media use can be used for the glory of God rather than to their detriment. As mentioned before, Paul says in 1 Corinthians 10:31, "So, whether you eat or drink, or whatever you do, do all to the glory of God." Our churches and youth ministries can be places where we can equip teenagers to use even their social media and technology for the glory of God.

Supporting parents by establishing technology guidelines at church

Another important way churches can support parents and help set up students for success is by establishing guidelines for technology during youth ministry functions. Often in our youth ministry, the adults in our church will come to observe our youth ministry, notice a few students on their phones during a youth gathering, and tell us that our teenagers are all addicted to their phones, or something like that. My response to these alarmed adults is challenging them to go to the main sanctuary on a Sunday and see if they don't notice the same with our adults. In fact, we all have probably noticed several people using their smartphones or tablets (hopefully for their Bible app) during a worship service. Of course, we hope that teenagers are exclusively using their phones for their Bible app during a youth group gathering, but it is not always true. And like teachers in schools, churches all notice the distraction these phones or tablets can be. In fact, from my (Danny's) viewpoint as a youth and family pastor, I often observed both adults and teenagers checking their devices for notifications or checking their Instagram accounts for "likes" they have received, both during and after worship services. Likewise, after worship services, we see people on their phones, and we notice it distracts from their social interactions with others.

Hence, this is a dilemma for churches and youth ministries regarding the use of devices at church. As parents, have we thought about this as well? Here are a few thoughts to ponder as we consider asking parents of teenagers, churches, and youth ministries to do what many schools are now beginning to do by having phones turned off during church gatherings.

Are our devices too distracting? We have seen increasing issues related to phone and social media use over the years. When we began in ministry nearly thirty years ago, there were no such things as smartphones or tablets (yes, we are old). We've seen the changes these devices have brought to the lives of adults and teenagers. Now, during worship or small group times, and even when people are interacting, it is rare not to see many people distracted by their devices. It is so common now to see people at church looking at their smartphones, students in the youth ministry checking text messages from friends or parents, or teenagers scrolling through social media during a small group time. Similarly, for example, when a student receives a smartphone notification, it distracts not only them but also others around them. At our church, we even had to train our adult leaders and student leaders not to turn on their phones right after our meetings ended so they could fellowship with others. Overall, if phones are too distracting for your church and youth ministry both during and after meetings, would your church consider banning their use inside the church?

Are we as the church giving approval to the persistent use of screens? There is no doubt that technology has content that causes negative consequences to the mental health crisis in the lives of teenagers. Moreover, families who try to moderate the use of it are having a hard time trying to navigate it. In addition, as noted earlier, researchers like Jonathan Haidt in his book *The Anxious Generation*, for example, have shown how social media and smartphone use are rewiring the minds of teenagers and has caused an increase in anxiety, depression, and self-harm. Perhaps churches and youth ministries could lead the way in showing there is an alternative way for social media and technology use and break the cycle of habitual use of it and the harm it causes.

Can our churches and youth ministry give alternate options to using screens? In our youth ministry, we budgeted to give new Bibles for those entering the middle school youth ministry. Likewise, if a newcomer came to our church and started attending regularly, we would purchase a Bible for them. Even for teenagers who forget their Bibles, we always have pew Bibles in the entrance to our meeting rooms. This can be an easy practice for adults as well. Overall, physical Bibles will naturally limit distractions from mobile devices at least during meetings. This also gives students and adults something to hold and withhold the temptation to check another app or email. Similarly, having a physical Bible can symbolically signify that God's Word is something of sacredness and value, rather than just a simple app.

Additionally, your youth ministry can also display a notice on a large screen before a meeting begins, asking everyone to turn off their phones during and after worship to minimize distraction, focus on worship, and encourage interaction and fellowship with others. Another important consideration is to start and end your youth ministry gatherings on time, especially for the sake of the parents and caregivers. We repeatedly hear teenagers tell us they must have their phones on because their parents need to leave early or must contact them potentially during the youth group time. For those issues, we would strongly encourage youth groups to communicate to parents and caregivers the start and end of youth ministry meetings and to be diligent to honor those times. This can develop a healthy relationship and trust with caregivers and reduces the need for endless texting about when their teenager will be finished at a youth group gathering or when they will be coming out to the car for a ride home. Youth groups can also use what some schools are doing for their classroom time and provide some sort of phone caddy for students' phones during youth group meetings, where they place them in the caddy before the meeting starts

Finally, we think it is important to communicate with each student the importance and value of their presence with Jesus and others in the youth group. A pastor friend in Houston constantly reminds students of their value and worth in Christ and how their presence and participation in the youth group are treasured by Jesus and by their youth ministry. Hence, it is his way of encouraging students to turn off their phones at church. It is a gospel-centered way to convey that each teenager's presence at youth group is valued and important, and thus not having their phone on is part of this.

Are youth ministries responding to the problems of cyberbullying and online abuse and exploitation? Even within our own churches and youth ministries, we must make it a safe place for teenagers to know that they can share and report online abuse. Years ago, we had a female student approach us very tentatively, sharing about a male student from youth group who contacted her on an online platform and asked her to send him some naked pictures of her. This was very shocking and hurtful to her. Frankly speaking, it was our first time ever dealing with anything like this, and we did not know what to do. Do I tell my church leadership? Do I inform her parents? Do I inform the parents of the other student? How do I confront the other student, yet also try to love that student in Christ? One of the most important things we ultimately did as a youth ministry and church was to tell our teenagers directly that our youth group was a place which had no tolerance for cyberbullying, online abuse, or exploitation. We welcomed them to tell any adult leader if any such situation were to arise with them or their friends.

Is technology impacting our church and our community to isolation? Our churches are meant to be a gathering of believers, as the body of Christ. Yet we know that our devices can create isolation as people stare at their screens instead of fellowshipping with one another. The Shema in Deuteronomy 6:4 is a call to a community of believers to walk and grow together in their faith. Churches and youth ministries must examine how their ministries are promoting and teaching this. Digital connections cannot replace real-life communities. Online friendships and relationships do not provide true intimacy or physical connectedness. Even the use of devices after church gatherings and worship services distracts our church community and genuine fellowship.

Promoting God-Glorifying Relationships

Ultimately, we are not alone in these concerns about screen use and social media, or in how to navigate their uses in our families, churches, and youth ministries. God has given us one another in the community of faith to navigate these challenging questions together. Still, there are not many easy or simple answers. What one church does will be different from another church. The same for parents. Each family will be different. Schools themselves are just beginning to ban or are considering banning phone use during school hours. But there are no easy answers for schools either. However, having continuing thoughts and conversations around healthy limits and usage of social media and devices is important. Teenagers and families must learn to see how technology might be detrimental or harmful. Churches and youth ministries can help families and teenagers think and work through these issues. We can promote God-glorifying relationships with social media and screen use at home and in the church.

CHAPTER 15

Take Heart: Resting in a New Identity

Sometimes as Christians in the church, our response to mental health challenges can be visceral, especially when it comes to teenagers. Because we know that teenagers are still developing mentally, physically, and spiritually, we may want to give them quick, pragmatic answers to their mental health struggles, as though they're something that can be easily overcome. For example, our reaction might be to tell them, "If you are a Christian, then a mental health issue means you're not trusting in God enough or your faith is weak. If you just learn how to trust God more, this problem will go away." Thus, we may have the tendency to view a teen's mental health struggle as solely a faith issue and seek easy, one-dimensional answers to it. On the other hand, we may be drawn to view their struggle as only a mental health issue, as though if we could just get them the right treatment, all of their difficulties would go away, without any attempt to understand the spiritual aspects of their struggle. Parents of teens with mental health issues often feel deep worry, hopelessness, and fear for their teenager, and so they (and church leaders) want to solve their problems as soon as possible.

One consequence of these perspectives is that it can lead to an overreliance on quick fixes. As parents, we might attempt to plug them into a small group or youth group activity, thinking that will relieve their anxiety or depression. Similarly, our youth leaders might offer to visit the students and talk with them, hoping a few conversations can sort everything out. Our youth pastors might offer to text the student Bible verses to encourage them. Or our churches might offer extra care for a student or tell them to reach out to us whenever they are feeling distress or sadness. None of these things are bad in themselves. However, only reaching for these quick, simple solutions can lead us to neglect deeper, more long-term ways we can help them mentally, physically, and spiritually.

Sometimes on long car drives, I (Danny) ask Monica every possible question I can think of about mental health. Over the years, these conversations have given me deeper insight into the complexities of the mental health struggles of teenagers, as well as the struggles their caregivers face in caring for them. These countless conversations have led me to realize that giving simple, pragmatic answers to mental health challenges is often unhelpful, but also that having a comprehensive understanding of the mysteries of mental health is impossible. As humans, we are finite, and we will never fully comprehend the brokenness of this world or the human mind. It reminds me of 1 Corinthians 13:12 when the apostle Paul says, "For now we see in a mirror dimly, but then face to face. Now I know in part; then I shall know fully, even as I have been fully known." Right now, our understanding of mental health, along with so many other things, is dim and partial. We must approach these complex issues with humility. At the same time, we must also hold onto the hope that someday we will clearly see and fully know the many things that confuse us in this world, and every tear will be wiped from our eyes (Revelation 21:4).

Until that day comes, we hope that our book will help you understand mental health issues in teens a little more deeply and care for them more faithfully and wisely. At the same time, as you engage in this work more intentionally, it is important to be prepared for the variety of ways each teen's story might work out. Over the years, we've seen the whole range of responses to our care for them. When we run into some of these teens as adults, we can see that they still have struggles but they are often thrilled to see us and even share openly about their ongoing mental health struggle. Others are more of a "success story" and are now living a stable, healthy life, both mentally and spiritually. Still others we never see or hear from again; we do not know what has happened to them or where they are today. Finally, there are those we see who give us more tepid responses, and we aren't sure why. We wonder if perhaps they didn't care for the help and love we once offered them.

God also calls churches and youth leaders to walk alongside the parents of hurting teenagers just as we care for their children. I'm reminded of one particular teen we encountered when I (Danny) was in my second year of youth ministry. We walked with her during her mental health breakdown in high school and we continued to minister to her parents as she went to college and into adulthood. Her struggles with mental health haunted her, and it was also a hardship for her parents.

We continue to see her parents at church, where they offer a gracious smile or a word of thanks to us for our many years of care. Families need the love and support of their local churches for the long haul as they walk through difficult experiences of mental health struggle.

Likewise, our call as parents is to patiently walk alongside these suffering teens for as long as that journey might take. Galatians 6:9 says, "And let us not grow weary of doing good, for in due season we will reap, if we do not give up." We might reap the reward of our efforts in this life when we see our teen who used to struggle with depression or anxiety begin to flourish as an adult, or we might reap it in heaven when we see our believing teenagers forever healed of their struggles (Revelation 21:4).

In John 16:33, as Jesus prepares his disciples for life without his physical presence, he says, "I have said these things to you, that in me you may have peace. In the world you will have tribulation. But take heart; I have overcome the world." Jesus acknowledges that our lives will be difficult. Yet he tells us to "take heart" because he has already overcome all of the things that trouble us. As we attempt to wisely try out various strategies for helping teenagers and their families, we must never lose sight of the importance of Jesus's gentle encouragement. This is the ultimate message of hope we can offer to teens and their parents—take heart, for Jesus has overcome the world, including the brokenness of our own hearts and minds.

Ultimately, when teenagers and their parents and caregivers are dealing with mental illness, this challenge may be short-term or it may be long-term, but if they are God's child, they can know this: In John 20, after Jesus's resurrection, he appears to his disciples and shows Thomas his scars. While this revelation was to help Thomas believe in him as the resurrected Savior, it was also to show them and us that while Jesus's scars were symbolic of his suffering and death, they were also to show us that he understands every pain we will ever face. Moreover, he was not only slain for us, but he was victorious for us, and as Thomas proclaims, he is "my Lord and my God." In the same way, as we care for our teenagers struggling with mental health, their identities (and yours as parents) might feel like they are wrapped up in their scars and pain. However, as parents, churches, and youth ministries, we point them to Jesus who gives them a new and greater identity than the weight of their mental health struggles. His death and resurrection on our behalf transform us into God's workmanship and righteousness, giving us all a new hope and new, true identity. This truth might not fully relieve our teens of their present struggles, but they can rest and trust in the truth that their hope and identity is not in the scars of their mental health struggles but in their new, greater identity in Christ.

Endnotes

Introduction

1. “Teen Mental Health Facts and Statistics,” Adolescent Wellness Academy, accessed June 15, 2024, https://adolescentwellnessacademy.com/teen-mental-health-facts-and-statistics/.

2. Sarah DeGue et al., “Mental Health, Suicidality, and Connectedness Among High School Students During the COVID-19 Pandemic — Adolescent Behaviors and Experiences Survey, United States, January–June 2021,” *MMWR*, Supplements 71, no. 3 (2022): 16–21, Centers for Disease Control and Prevention, https://www.cdc.gov/mmwr/volumes/71/su/su7103a3.htm.

3. Iliana Garcia and Jean O’Neil, “Anxiety in Adolescents,” *The Journal for Nurse Practitioners* 17, no. 1 (2021): 49–53, https://doi.org/10.1016/j.nurpra.2020.08.021.

4. Sally Curtin and Matthew Garnett, “Suicide Mortality in the United States, 2001–2021,” NCHS Data Brief, no. 464 (2023), https://www.cdc.gov/nchs/data/databriefs/db464.pdf.

5. Arianna Prothero, “Teen Suicides Rising Sharply, Federal Data Shows,” *Education Week*, October 17, 2019, https://www.edweek.org/leadership/teen-suicides-rising-sharply-federal-data-show/2019/10.

6. Prothero, “Teen Suicides.”

7. “Mental health of adolescents,” World Health Organization, October 10, 2024, https://www.who.int/news-room/fact-sheets/detail/adolescent-mental-health.

8. David Powlison, *Take Heart: Daily Devotions to Deepen Your Faith* (New Growth Press, 2022), 12.

Chapter 1

1. “Mental Illness,” National Institute of Mental Health, accessed August 10, 2024, https://www.nimh.nih.gov/health/statistics/mental-illness.

2. For a comprehensive listing of psychiatric disorders, see the American Psychiatric Association’s *Diagnostic and Statistical Manual of Mental Disorders*, 5th ed. (American Psychiatric Association, 2022).

3. John Calvin, *Institutes of the Christian Religion*, trans. Henry Beveridge (Hendrickson Publishers, 2008), II.2.15.

4. "The Confessional Statement of the Biblical Counseling Coalition," Biblical Counseling Coalition, accessed August 23, 2024, https://www.biblicalcounselingcoalition.org/confessional-statement/.

5. Timothy Keller, "Four Models of Counseling in Pastoral Ministry," Gospel In Life, May 12, 2010, https://gospelinlife.com/manual-paper/four-models-of-counseling-in-pastoral-ministry/.

6. Nate Brooks et al., "What Is Redemptive Counseling / Clinically Informed Biblical Counseling?" accessed June 5, 2024, https://www.sebts.edu/wp-content/uploads/2024/07/What-is-RCCIBC.pdf.

Chapter 3

1. Kerstin Konrad et al., "Brain Development During Adolescence: Neuroscientific Insights Into this Developmental Period," *Deutsches Ärzteblatt International* 110, no. 25 (2013): 425, https://doi.org/10.3238/arztebl.2013.0425.

2. BJ Casey et al., "Beyond Simple Models of Adolescence to An Integrated Circuit-based account: A commentary," *Developmental Cognitive Neuroscience* 17 (February 2016): 128–130, https://doi.org/10.1016/j.dcn.2015.12.006.

3. "The Youth Risk Behavior Survey Data Summary & Trends Report: 2013–2023," Centers for Disease Control and Prevention, accessed June 10, 2024, https://www.cdc.gov/yrbs/dstr/index.html.

4. BJ Casey et al., "Treating the Developing versus Developed Brain: Translating Preclinical Mouse and Human Studies," *Neuron* 86, no. 6 (2015): 1358–1368. Used with permission.

5. "Data and Statistics on Children's Mental Health," Centers for Disease Control and Prevention, accessed July 2, 2024, https://www.cdc.gov/children-mental-health/data-research/?CDC_AAref_Val=https://www.cdc.gov/childrensmentalhealth/data.html.

6. "Mental Health by the Numbers," National Alliance on Mental Illness, accessed July 23, 2024, https://www.nami.org/about-mental-illness/mental-health-by-the-numbers/.

7. Frank Paulus, et al., "Emotional Dysregulation in Children and Adolescents With Psychiatric Disorders. A Narrative Review," *Front. Psychiatry* 12, no. 628252 (2021), https://doi.org/10.3389/fpsyt.2021.628252; Johanna Özlem Schäfer et al., "Emotion Regulation Strategies in Depressive and Anxiety Symptoms in Youth: A Meta-Analytic Review," *Journal of Youth and Adolescence* 46, no. 2 (2017): 261–276, https://doi.org/10.1007/s10964-016-0585-0; Katherine Young et al., "Positive and Negative Emotion Regulation in Adolescence: Links to Anxiety and Depression," *Brain Sciences* 9, no. 4 (2019): 76. https://doi.org/10.3390/brainsci9040076.

8. "Gender Dysphoria Statistics In The United States," Bright Path Behavioral Health, December 3, 2024, https://www.brightpathbh.com/gender-dysphoria-statistics/.

9. For more helpful discussion about this topic, we recommend *Grounded in Grace* by Jonathan Holmes (New Growth Press, 2024).

10. "Loneliness in young people: research briefing," Mental Health Foundation, accessed March 26, 2025, https://www.mentalhealth.org.uk/our-work/public-engagement/unlock-loneliness/loneliness-young-people-research-briefing.

11. Jasmin Tahmaseb-McConatha, "Technology Use, Loneliness, and Isolation," *Psychology Today*, October 19, 2022, https://www.psychologytoday.com/us/blog/live-long-and-prosper/202210/technology-use-loneliness-and-isolation.

12. Annie Flanagan and Matt Richtel, "'It's Life or Death': The Mental Health Crisis Among U.S. Teens," *The New York Times*, April 23, 2022, https://www.nytimes.com/2022/04/23/health/mental-health-crisis-teens.html.

13. Jean Twenge, *Generations: The Real Differences Between Gen Z, Millennials, Gen X, Boomers, and Silents—and What They Mean for America's Future* (Atria Books, 2023), 502–504.

14. "Why The Decline in Church Attendance is a Public Health Crisis," *ChurchTrac*, accessed March 25, 2025, https://www.churchtrac.com/articles/why-the-decline-in-church-attendance-is-a-public-health-crisis.

Chapter 4

1. Christoph Flückiger et al., "The Alliance in Adult Psychotherapy: A Meta-Analytic Synthesis," *Psychotherapy* 55, no. 4 (2018): 316–340, https://doi.org/10.1037/pst0000172.

2. Tamara Dimic et al., "Young people's experience of the therapeutic alliance: A systematic review," *Clinical Psychology & Psychotherapy* 30, no. 6 (2023): 1482–1511, https://doi.org/10.1002/cpp.2885.

3. Dimic et al., "Young people's experience."

4. Dimic et al., "Young people's experience."

5. Dimic et al., "Young people's experience."

6. Dimic et al., "Young people's experience."

7. Clara Hill, *Helping Skills: Facilitating Exploration, Insight, and Action* (American Psychological Association, 2019).

Chapter 5

1. Sanjay Gupta, host, *Chasing Life*, podcast, episode 457, "Is There a College Mental Health Crisis?," CNN Audio, September 6, 2024, https://www.cnn.com/audio/podcasts/chasing-life/episodes/a84c33d0-37bb-11ef-8219-4f0967ee8eba

2. Chap Clark, "In Spite of How They Act," *Decision*, August 17, 2004, https://decisionmagazine.com/in-spite-of-how-they-act/.

3. Ronald Butzlaff and Jill Hooley, "Expressed emotion and psychiatric relapse: a meta-analysis," *Archives of General Psychiatry* 55, no. 6 (June 1998): 547–52, doi:10.1001/archpsyc.55.6.547.

Chapter 6

1. Basyle Tchividjian and Shira M. Berkovitis, *The Child Safeguarding Policy Guide for Churches and Ministries* (New Growth Press, 2017).

Chapter 7

1. Todd Hare et al., "Biological Substrates of Emotional Reactivity and Regulation in Adolescence During an Emotional Go-Nogo Task," *Biological Psychiatry* 63, no. 10 (2008): 927–34, https://doi.org/10.1016/j.biopsych.2008.03.015.

2. Hare et al., "Biological substrates of emotional reactivity and regulation."

3. Kathleen Ries Merikangas et al., "Lifetime prevalence of mental disorders in U.S. adolescents: results from the National Comorbidity Survey Replication—Adolescent Supplement (NCS-A)," *Journal of the American Academy of Child & Adolescent Psychiatry* 49, no. 10 (2010): 980–9, https://doi.org/10.1016/j.jaac.2010.05.017.

4. Joseph Biederman et al., "Further Evidence of Association Between Behavioral Inhibition and Social Anxiety in Children," *American Journal of Psychiatry* 158, no. 10 (2001): 1673–9, https://doi.org/10.1176/appi.ajp.158.10.1673.

5. Nicholas Allan et al., "Developmental Trajectories of Anxiety Symptoms in Early Adolescence: The Influence of Anxiety Sensitivity," *Journal of Abnormal Child Psychology* 42, no. 4 (2014): 589–600, https://doi.org/10.1007/s10802-013-9806-0.

6. Monica Kim, "Waves" handout. Used with permission.

7. Monica Kim, "Thoughts and Feelings on Leaves." Used with permission.

8. Monica Kim, "Taking Care of Today" handout. Used with permission.

9. María Rodriguez-Ayllon et al., "Role of Physical Activity and Sedentary Behavior in the Mental Health of Preschoolers, Children and Adolescents: A Systematic Review and Meta-Analysis," *Sports Medicine* 49, no. 9 (2019): 1383–1410, https://doi.org/10.1007/s40279-019-01099-5.

10. Matthew Blake et al., "Mechanisms underlying the association between insomnia, anxiety, and depression in adolescence: Implications for behavioral sleep interventions," *Clinical Psychology Review* 63 (2017): 25–40, https://doi.org/10.1016/j.cpr.2018.05.006; Margaret Fitzpatrick et al., "Relationship Between Family and Friend Support and Psychological Distress in Adolescents," *Journal of Pediatric Health Care* 38, no. 6 (2024): 804–11. https://doi.org/10.1016/j.pedhc.2024.06.016.

11. Kenisha Russell Jonsson et al., "Associations between dietary behaviours and the mental and physical well-being of Swedish adolescents,"

Child and Adolescent Psychiatry and Mental Health 18, no. 43 (2024), https://doi.org/10.1186/s13034-024-00733-z; Julia Dabravolskaj et al., "Association Between Diet and Mental Health Outcomes in a Sample of 13,887 Adolescents in Canada," *Preventing Chronic Disease* 21, no. 82 (2024), http://dx.doi.org/10.5888/pcd21.240187.

12. Robert Spitzer et al., "A Brief Measure for Assessing Generalized Anxiety Disorder: The GAD-7," *Archives of Internal Medicine* 166, no. 10 (2006): 1092–7, https://doi.org/10.1001/archinte.166.10.1092.

Chapter 8

1. Jennifer Jackson et al., "Expression of Anger in Depressed Adolescents: The Role of the Family Environment," *Journal of Abnormal Child Psychology* 39, no. 3 (2011): 463–74. https://doi.org/10.1007/s10802-010-9473-3.

2. Sylia Wilson and Nathalie Dumornay, "Rising Rates of Adolescent Depression in the United States: Challenges and Opportunities in the 2020s," *The Journal of Adolescent Health* 70, no. 3 (2022): 354–5. https://doi.org/10.1016/j.jadohealth.2021.12.003.

3. Olivia Sappenfield et al., "National Survey of Children's Health: Adolescent Mental and Behavioral Health, 2023," HRSA, October 2024, https://mchb.hrsa.gov/sites/default/files/mchb/data-research/nsch-data-brief-adolescent-mental-behavioral-health-2023.pdf.

4. "Key Substance Use and Mental Health Indicators in the United States: Results from the 2021 National Survey on Drug Use and Health," Substance Abuse and Mental Health Services Administration, Center for Behavioral Health Statistics and Quality, Substance Abuse and Mental Health Services Administration, accessed April 24, 2025, https://www.samhsa.gov/data/sites/default/files/reports/rpt39443/2021NSDUHNNR122322/2021NSDUHNNR122322.htm.

5. Jess Shatkin, *Child & Adolescent Mental Health: A Practical, All-in-One Guide*, 3rd ed. (Norton Professional Books, 2024).

6. Patrick Sullivan et al., "Genetic Epidemiology of Major Depression: Review and Meta-Analysis." *The American Journal of Psychiatry* 157, no. 10 (2000): 1552–62, https://doi.org/10.1176/appi.ajp.157.10.1552; Kenneth Kendler et al., "A Swedish National Twin Study of Lifetime Major Depression," *The American Journal of Psychiatry* 163, no. 1 (2006): 109–14, https://doi.org/10.1176/appi.ajp.163.1.109.

7. Roselind Lieb et al., "Parental Major Depression and the Risk of Depression and Other Mental Disorders in Offspring: A Prospective-Longitudinal Community Study," *Archives of General Psychiatry* 59, no. 4 (2002): 365–74, https://doi.org/10.1001/archpsyc.59.4.365.

8. Myrna Weissman et al. "Offspring of Depressed Parents: 20 Years Later," *The American Journal of Psychiatry* 163, no. 6 (2006), 1001–8, https://doi.org/10.1176/ajp.2006.163.6.1001

9. Monica Kim, "Thoughts and Feelings on Leaves." Used with permission.

10. Monica Kim, "What Does Depression Say About Who God Is and Who I Am" handout. Used with permission.

11. Monica Kim, "Engaging Social Support" handout. Used with permission.

12. Monica Kim, "What Does Depression Say."

13. María Rodriguez-Ayllon et al., "Role of Physical Activity and Sedentary Behavior in the Mental Health of Preschoolers, Children and Adolescents: A Systematic Review and Meta-Analysis," *Sports Medicine* 49, no. 9 (2019): 1383–1410, https://doi.org/10.1007/s40279-019-01099-5.

14. Anne-Laura van Harmelen et al., "Friendships and Family Support Reduce Subsequent Depressive Symptoms in At-Risk Adolescents," *PLOS One* 11, no. 5 (2016), https://doi.org/10.1371/journal.pone.0153715; Margaret Fitzpatrick et al., "Relationship Between Family and Friend Support and Psychological Distress in Adolescents," *Journal of Pediatric Health Care* 38, no. 6 (2024): 804–11, https://doi.org/10.1016/j.pedhc.2024.06.016

15. Kenisha Russell Jonsson et al., "Associations between dietary behaviours and the mental and physical well-being of Swedish adolescents," *Child and Adolescent Psychiatry and Mental Health* 18, no. 43 (2024), https://doi.org/10.1186/s13034-024-00733-z; Julia Dabravolskaj et al., "Association Between Diet and Mental Health Outcomes in a Sample of 13,887 Adolescents in Canada," *Preventing Chronic Disease* 21, no. 82 (Oct. 2024). http://dx.doi.org/10.5888/pcd21.240187.

16. "Teen Depression: More Than Just Moodiness," National Institute of Mental Health, accessed April 24, 2025, https://www.nimh.nih.gov/sites/default/files/documents/health/publications/teen-depression/Teen_Depression_More_Than_Just_Moodiness_2022.pdf.

17. Robert Spitzer et al., "A brief Measure for Assessing Generalized Anxiety Disorder: The GAD-7," *Archives of Internal Medicine* 166, no. 10 (2006): 1092–7, https://doi.org/10.1001/archinte.166.10.1092.

Chapter 9

1. Michaela Bucchianeri et al., "Body dissatisfaction: Do associations with disordered eating and psychological well-being differ across race/ethnicity in adolescent girls and boys?," *Cultural Diversity & Ethnic Minority Psychology* 22, no. 1 (2016): 137–46, https://doi.org/10.1037/cdp0000036; Shirley Wang et al., "Fifteen-Year Prevalence, Trajectories, and Predictors of Body Dissatisfaction From Adolescence to Middle Adulthood," *Clinical Psychological Science* 7, no. 6 (2019): 1403–1415, https://doi.org/10.1177/2167702619859331.

2. Jess Shatkin, *Child & Adolescent Mental Health: A Practical, All-in-One Guide,* 3rd ed. (Norton Professional Books, 2024).

3. Donald McCreary and Doris Sasse, "An Exploration of the Drive for Muscularity in Adolescent Boys and Girls," *Journal of American College Health* 48, no. 6 (2000): 297–304, https://doi.org/10.1080/07448480009596271.

4. Michaela Bucchianeri et al., "Body dissatisfaction."

5. American Psychiatric Association, *Diagnostic and Statistical Manual of Mental Disorders*, 5th ed. (American Psychiatric Association, 2022), 95.

6. Sonja Swanson et al., "Prevalence and correlates of eating disorders in adolescents. Results from the national comorbidity survey replication adolescent supplement," *Archives of General Psychiatry* 68, no. 7 (2011): 714–23. doi:10.1001/archgenpsychiatry.2011.22.

7. Sonja Swanson et al., "Prevalence and correlates of eating disorders in adolescents."

8. Katherine Halmi et al., "Unique features associated with age of onset of anorexia nervosa," *Psychiatry Research* 1, no. 2 (1979): 209–15, doi:10.1016/0165-1781(79)90063-5; Nadia Micali et al., "The incidence of eating disorders in the UK in 2000–2009: findings from the General Practice Research Database," *BMJ Open* 3, no. 5 (2013): doi:10.1136/bmjopen-2013-002646.

9. Sarah Barakat et al., "Risk factors for eating disorders: findings from a rapid review," *Journal of Eating Disorders* 11, no. 8 (2023): doi:10.1186/s40337-022-00717-4.

10. "Eating Disorders: What You Need to Know," National Institute of Mental Health, accessed January 15, 2025, https://www.nimh.nih.gov/health/publications/eating-disorders; Jess Shatkin, *Child & Adolescent Mental Health*.

11. "Eating Disorders," National Institute of Mental Health.

12. "Eating Disorders," National Institute of Mental Health; Jess Shatkin, *Child & Adolescent Mental Health*.

13. Laura Murphy, "What to Say, What Not to Say," training, Drexel University Counseling Center, Philadelphia, PA, January 27, 2021. Used with permission.

14. Edward T. Welch, *Eating Disorders: The Quest for Thinness* (New Growth Press, 2008).

15. Monica Kim, "Negative Thoughts and Feelings About My Body on Leaves in a River Floating to Jesus" worksheet. Used with permission.

16. Adrian Paterna et al., "Internalization of body shape ideals and body dissatisfaction: A systematic review and meta-analysis," *International Journal of Eating Disorders* 54, no. 9 (2021): 1575–1600, https://doi.org/10.1002/eat.23568.

17. Monica Kim, "Made in God's Image: Fearfully and Wonderfully Made" handout. Used with permission.

18. Helen Thai et al., "Reducing social media use improves appearance and weight esteem in youth with emotional distress," *Psychology of Popular Media* 13, no. 1 (2023): 162–9, https://doi.org/10.1037/ppm0000460.

19. Jess Shatkin, *Child & Adolescent Mental Health*; "Eating Disorders," National Institute of Mental Health.

20. Jess Shatkin, *Child & Adolescent Mental Health*; "Eating Disorders," National Institute of Mental Health.

Chapter 10

1. "The Youth Risk Behavior Survey Data Summary & Trends Report: 2013–2023," Centers for Disease Control and Prevention, accessed June 10, 2024, https://www.cdc.gov/yrbs/dstr/index.html.

2. SAMHSA, "2023 National Survey on Drug Use and Health," Table 2.9A—Alcohol, binge alcohol, and heavy alcohol use in past month: among persons aged 12 or older; by detailed age category, numbers in thousands, 2022 and 2023, 2024, https://www.samhsa.gov/data/report/2023-nsduh-detailed-tables.

3. Ken Winters and Amelia Arria, "Adolescent Brain Development and Drugs," *The Prevention Researcher* 18, no. 2 (2011): 21–4.

4. Jess Shatkin, *Child & Adolescent Mental Health: A Practical, All-in-One Guide,* 3rd ed. (Norton Professional Books, 2024).

5. "Key substance use and mental health indicators in the United States: Results from the 2023 National Survey on Drug Use and Health," Substance Abuse and Mental Health Services Administration, Center for Behavioral Health Statistics and Quality, Substance Abuse and Mental Health Services Administration, accessed June 23, 2024, https://www.samhsa.gov/data/report/2023-nsduh-annual-national-report.

6. "Key substance use and mental health indicators," SAMHSA.

7. Jonathan Schaefer et al., "Associations between adolescent cannabis use and young-adult functioning in three longitudinal twin studies," *Proceedings of the National Academy of Sciences of the United States of America* 118, no. 14 (2021), https://doi.org/10.1073/pnas.2013180118.

8. George King et al., "Neuropsychological deficits in adolescent methamphetamine abusers," *Psychopharmacology* 212, no. 2 (2010). https://doi.org/10.1007/s00213-010-1949-x; Sophia Luikinga et al., "Developmental perspectives on methamphetamine abuse: Exploring adolescent vulnerabilities on brain and behavior," *Progress in Neuro-Psychopharmacology and Biological Psychiatry* 87 (2018): 78–84, https://doi.org/10.1016/j.pnpbp.2017.11.010.

9. Tammy Chung et al., "Adolescent Binge Drinking," *Alcohol Research: Current Reviews* 39, no. 1 (2018): 5–15; Sandra Brown and Susan Tapert, "Adolescence and the Trajectory of Alcohol Use: Basic to Clinical Studies," *Annals of the New York Academy of Sciences* 1021, no. 1 (2006): 234–44, https://doi.org/10.1196/annals.1308.028.

10. Nora Volkow et al., "Prevalence of Substance Use Disorders by Time Since First Substance Use Among Young People in the US," *JAMA Pediatrics* 175, no. 6 (2021): 640–3, doi:10.1001/jamapediatrics.2020.6981.

11. "Scalable Surveillance of E-Cigarette Products on Instagram and TikTok Using Computer Vision," Nicotine & Tobacco Research, accessed August 25, 2024, https://academic.oup.com/ntr/article/26/5/552/7382253.

12. Scott Donaldson et al., "Online Purchase Attempts of Flavored E-Cigarettes to Minors in California Before and After Senate Bill 793," *JAMA Network Open* 6, no. 12 (2023), doi: 10.1001/jamanetworkopen.2023.48749.

13. Tara Woodward et al., "Risk & protective factors for youth substance use across family, peers, school, & leisure domains," *Children and Youth Services Review* 151 (2023), https://doi.org/10.1016/j.childyouth.2023.107027.

14. Alison Bryant et al., "How Academic Achievement, Attitudes, and Behaviors Relate to the Course of Substance Use During Adolescence: A 6-Year, Multiwave National Longitudinal Study," *Journal of Research on Adolescence* 13, no. 3 (2003): 361–97, https://doi.org/10.1111/1532-7795.1303005.

15. Flavio Francisco Marsiglia et al., "God forbid! Substance use among religious and nonreligious youth," *American Journal of Orthopsychiatry* 75, no. 4 (2005): 585–98, https://doi.org/10.1037/0002-9432.75.4.585.

16. Chloe Jordan and Susan Andersen, "Sensitive periods of substance abuse: Early risk for the transition to dependence," *Developmental Cognitive Neuroscience*, 25 (2017): 29–44, https://doi.org/10.1016/j.dcn.2016.10.004.

17. Monica Kim, "Conflicting Thoughts and Feelings About My Substance Use: Crying Out to God" handout. Used with permission.

Chapter 11

1. American Psychiatric Association, *Diagnostic and Statistical Manual of Mental Disorders,* 5th ed. (American Psychiatric Association, 2022).

2. APA, *Diagnostic and Statistical Manual.*

3. Jess Shatkin, *Child & Adolescent Mental Health: A Practical, All-in-One Guide,* 3rd ed. (Norton Professional Books, 2024).

4. Monica Kim, "Thoughts, Feelings, and Trauma Memories on Leaves" handout. Used with permission; Monica Kim, "Thoughts, Feelings, and Trauma Memories: Crying Out to God" handout. Used with permission.

5. Melissa Polusny et al., "Effects of parents' experiential avoidance and PTSD on adolescent disaster-related posttraumatic stress symptomatology," *Journal of Family Psychology* 25, no. 2 (2011): 220, https://psycnet.apa.org/doi/10.1037/a0022945.

6. Erin Koffel et al., "Sleep Disturbances in Posttraumatic Stress Disorder: Updated Review and Implications for Treatment," *Psychiatric Annals* 46, no. 3 (2016): 173–6, https://doi.org/10.3928/00485713-20160125-01.

7. Lauren Hale et al., "Youth Screen Media Habits and Sleep: Sleep-Friendly Screen Behavior Recommendations for Clinicians, Educators, and Parents," *Child and Adolescent Psychiatric Clinics of North America* 27, no. 2 (2018): 229–45, https://doi.org/10.1016/j.chc.2017.11.014.

Chapter 12

1. American Psychiatric Association, *Diagnostic and Statistical Manual of Mental Disorders*, 5th ed. (American Psychiatric Association, 2022).

2. Philip Gorwood et al., "Gender and age at onset in schizophrenia: impact of family history," *American Journal of Psychiatry* 152, no. 2 (February 1995): 208–12. https://doi.org/10.1176/ajp.152.2.208.

3. Alastair Cardno and Irving Gottesman, "Twin studies of schizophrenia: from bow-and-arrow concordances to star wars Mx and functional genomics," *American Journal of Medical Genetics* 97, no. 1 (2001): 12–7, https://doi.org/10.1002/(SICI)1096-8628(200021)97:1<12::AID-AJMG3>3.0.CO;2-U.

4. Jess Shatkin, *Child & Adolescent Mental Health: A Practical, All-in-One Guide,* 3rd ed. (Norton Professional Books, 2024).

5. Jon McClellan et al., "Practice Parameter for the Assessment and Treatment of Children and Adolescents with Schizophrenia," *Journal of the American Academy of Child and Adolescent Psychiatry* 52, no. 9 (2013): 976–90, https://doi.org/10.1016/j.jaac.2013.02.008.

6. Michael Goldstein et al., "Patterns of Expressed Emotion and Patient Coping Styles that Characterise the Families of Recent Onset Schizophrenics," *British Journal of Psychiatry* 155, no. 5 (1989): 107–11, https://doi.org/10.1192/S0007125000296074.

7. Goldstein et al., "Patterns of Expressed Emotion."

8. Jennifer Lish et al., "The National Depressive and Manic-depressive Association (DMDA) survey of bipolar members," *Journal of Affective Disorders* 31, no. 4 (1994): 281–94, https://doi.org/10.1016/0165-0327(94)90104-X.

9. Peter Lewinsohn et al., "Bipolar disorder during adolescence and young adulthood in a community sample," *Bipolar Disorders* 2, no. 3p2 (2000): 281–93, https://doi.org/10.1034/j.1399-5618.2000.20309.x.

10. Lesley Arnold, "Gender differences in bipolar disorder," *Psychiatric Clinics of North America* 26, no. 3 (2003): 595–620, https://doi.org/10.1016/S0193-953X(03)00036-4.

11. Gustavo Vázquez et al., "Recurrence rates in bipolar disorder: Systematic comparison of long-term prospective, naturalistic studies versus randomized controlled trials," *European Neuropsychopharmacology* 25, no. 10 (2015): 1501–12. https://doi.org/10.1016/j.euroneuro.2015.07.013; Carlotta Cirone et al., "What Do We Know about the Long-Term Course of Early Onset Bipolar Disorder? A Review of the Current Evidence," *Brain Sciences* 11, no. 3 (2021), https://doi.org/10.3390/brainsci11030341.

12. Benjamin Goldstein et al., "The International Society for Bipolar Disorders Task Force report on pediatric bipolar disorder: Knowledge to date and directions for future research," *Bipolar Disorders* 19, no. 7 (2017): 524–43, https://doi.org/10.1111/bdi.12556.

13. Jennifer Barnett and Jordan Smoller, "The genetics of bipolar disorder," *Neuroscience* 164, no. 1 (2009): 331–43, https://doi.org/10.1016/j.neuroscience.2009.03.080.

14. Stacey McCraw et al., "The duration of undiagnosed bipolar disorder: Effect on outcomes and treatment response," *Journal of Affective Disorders* 168, no. 15 (2014): 422–9, https://doi.org/10.1016/j.jad.2014.07.025.

15. Kevin Connolly and Michael Thase, "The Clinical Management of Bipolar Disorder: A Review of Evidence-Based Guidelines," *Primary Care Companion for CNS Disorders* 13, no. 4 (2011), https://doi.org/10.4088/PCC.10r01097.

16. Jon McClellan et al., "Practice Parameter for the Assessment and Treatment of Children and Adolescents With Bipolar Disorder," *Journal of the American Academy of Child and Adolescent Psychiatry* 46, no. 1 (2007): 107–25, https://doi.org/10.1097/01.chi.0000242240.69678.c4.

17. Colleen Cummings and Mary Fristad, "Pediatric bipolar disorder: recognition in primary care," *Current Opinion in Pediatrics* 20, no. 5 (2008): 560–5, doi:10.1097/MOP.0b013e32830fe3d2.

18. Benjamin Goldstein et al., "The International Society for Bipolar Disorders Task Force report."

19. Anekal Amaresha and Ganesan Venkatasubramanian, "Expressed emotion in schizophrenia: an overview," *Indian Journal of Psychological Medicine* 34, no. 1 (2012): 12–20, https://doi.org/10.4103/0253-7176.96149.

20. Neal Stolar, "Cognitive Therapy for the Treatment of Psychosis/Schizophrenia," training, Drexel University Counseling Center, Philadelphia, PA, April 8, 2021.

21. Anna Sunshine and Jon McClellan, "Practitioner Review: Psychosis in children and adolescents," *Journal of Child Psychology and Psychiatry* 64, no. 7 (2023): 980–8, https://doi.org/10.1111/jcpp.13777; Hope Gillette, "What Are Common Schizophrenia Symptoms in Teens?," *Healthline*, April 4, 2023, https://www.healthline.com/health/schizophrenia/schizophrenia-symptoms-in-teens#symptoms; Chris Hollis, "Schizophrenia in children and adolescents," *BJPsych Advances* 21, no. 5 (2015): 333–41, https://doi.org/10.1192/apt.bp.114.014076; "Schizophrenia," National Institute of Mental Health, U.S. Department of Health and Human Services, National Institutes of Health, accessed April 29, 2025, https://www.nimh.nih.gov/health/topics/schizophrenia.

22. "Bipolar Disorder in Teens and Young Adults: Know the Signs," National Institute of Mental Health, accessed April 29, 2025, https://www.nimh.nih.gov/health/publications/bipolar-disorder-in-teens-and-young-adults-know-the-signs.

23. "Bipolar Disorder," National Institute of Mental Health; Jess Shatkin, *Child & Adolescent Mental Health: A Practical, All-in-One Guide,* 3rd ed. (New York, Norton Professional Books, 2024).

24. "Bipolar Disorder," National Institute of Mental Health.
25. "Bipolar Disorder," National Institute of Mental Health.

Chapter 13

1. "2023 NSDUH Annual National Report," Substance Abuse and Mental Health Services Administration (SAMHSA), accessed June 23, 2024, https://www.samhsa.gov/data/report/2023-nsduh-annual-national-report.

2. Jess Shatkin, *Child & Adolescent Mental Health: A Practical, All-in-One Guide,* 3rd ed. (Norton Professional Books, 2024).

3. Sally Curtin, "State Suicide Rates Among Adolescents and Young Adults Aged 10–24: United States, 2000–2018," *National Vital Statistics Reports* 69 (11): 104.

4. "Health Disparities in Suicide," Centers for Disease Control and Prevention, accessed September 3, 2024, https://www.cdc.gov/suicide/disparities/index.html.

5. "Health Disparities in Suicide," CDC.

6. Jess Shatkin, *Child & Adolescent Mental Health.*

7. "Navigating a Mental Health Crisis," National Alliance of Mental Illness, accessed July 28, 2004, https://www.nami.org/support-education/publications-reports/guides/navigating-a-mental-health-crisis/?gad_source=1&gclid=Cj0KCQjwu-63BhC9ARIsAMMTLXRAbPwmRwlFKJxaqOiolj9iMlfvdrO8mr52GpLMa3rOug8e8K_ejAUaAmfSEALw_wcB.

8. Elisha Galaif et al., "Suicidality, depression, and alcohol use among adolescents: a review of empirical findings," *International Journal of Adolescent Medicine and Health* 19, no. 1 (2007): 27–35, https://doi.org/10.1515/ijamh.2007.19.1.27.

9. "Empowering Schools, Campuses & Communities to Prevent Suicide & Violence with The Columbia Protocol," The Columbia Lighthouse Project, accessed July 12, 2024, https://cssrs.columbia.edu/wp-content/uploads/C-SSRS-Brochure-for-Education-1.pdf.

10. "Suicide Safety Plan," accessed August 24, 2024, https://suicidesafetyplan.app/.

11. "Empowering Schools, Campuses & Communities," The Columbia Lighthouse Project.

Chapter 14

1. "Parents Under Pressure," U.S. Department of Health and Human Services, accessed August 26, 2024, https://www.hhs.gov/sites/default/files/parents-under-pressure.pdf.

2. "Explicit content, time-wasting are key social media worries for parents of U.S. teens," Pew Research Center, December 15, 2022, https://www.pewresearch.org/short-reads/2022/12/15/explicit-content-time-wasting-are-key-social-media-worries-for-parents-of-u-s-teens/.

3. "Internet addiction disorder: When technology becomes a problem," *European Psychiatry* 64, no. 1 (2021), https://doi.org/10.1192/j.eurpsy.2021.1703.

4. Ronald Pies, "Should DSM-V Designate 'Internet Addiction' a Mental Disorder?" *Psychiatry (Edgmont)* 6, no. 2 (2009): 31–37: https://pmc.ncbi.nlm.nih.gov/articles/PMC2719452/.

5. Jean Twenge, *iGen: Why Today's Super-Connected Kids Are Growing Up Less Rebellious, More Tolerant, Less Happy—and Completely Unprepared for Adulthood—and What That Means for the Rest of Us* (Atria Paperback, 2017), 459.

6. "Social Media and Youth Mental Health," U.S. Department of Health and Human Services, accessed August 3, 2024, https://www.hhs.gov/surgeongeneral/priorities/youth-mental-health/social-media/index.html.

7. "Social Media," U.S. Department of Health and Human Services.

8. "Social Media," U.S. Department of Health and Human Services.

9. "72% of U.S. high school teachers say cellphone distraction is a major problem in the classroom," Pew Research Center, June 12, 2024. https://www.pewresearch.org/short-reads/2024/06/12/72-percent-of-us-high-school-teachers-say-cellphone-distraction-is-a-major-problem-in-the-classroom/.